Things Happen When Women Care

Emilie Barnes

HARVEST HOUSE PUBLISHERS
Eugene, Oregon 97402

Except where otherwise indicated, all Scripture quotations in this book are taken from the New American Standard Bible, Copyright © 1960, 1962, 1963, 1968, 1971, 1972, 1973, 1975, 1977 by The Lockman Foundation. Used by permission.

Verses marked NIV are taken from the Holy Bible, New International Version, Copyright © 1973, 1978, 1984 by the International Bible Society. Used by permission of Zondervan Bible Publishers.

Verses marked TLB are taken from The Living Bible, Copyright © 1971 owned by assignment by Illinois Regional Bank N.A. (as trustee). Used by permission of Tyndale House Publishers, Inc., Wheaton, Illinois 60189. All rights reserved.

THINGS HAPPEN WHEN WOMEN CARE

Copyright © 1990 Harvest House Publishers
Eugene, Oregon 97402

Library of Congress Cataloging-in-Publication Data

Barnes, Emilie
    Things happen when women care: hospitality and friendship in today's busy world / Emilie Barnes.
    ISBN 0-89081-837-1
    1. Women—Religious life.   2. Women—Conduct of life.   3. Home economics.   I. Title.
    BV4527.B36   1990   90-35983
    248.8'—dc20   CIP

All rights reserved. No portion of this book may be reproduced in any form without the written permission of the Publisher.

Printed in the United States of America.

———————— ♥ ————————

This book is dedicated to all the women who have written to tell me how the "More Hours in My Day" ministry has challenged their lives and encouraged them to take action. These women have either attended one of my seminars or read one of my books and responded to God's challenge.

I appreciate very much these women taking time from their busy schedules to write me. These letters are such an affirmation to me and my ministry to the women in America and Canada. Without these women, this book would not have been possible.

I also dedicate this book to Eileen Mason, editor-in-chief of Harvest House Publishers, for encouraging me to write on this topic. She has been such a caring person, and I certainly appreciate her stimulation.

A special dedication goes to you women who read this book and respond to its challenge. May we reflect God's love to a hurting world by caring for people. Sometimes we are the only Bible that people will read. We are to be seasoning and fragrance to those around us.

—Emilie Barnes

———————— ♥ ————————

Contents

———— ♥ ————

———— ♥ ————

More Hours In My Day can provide many of the organizational materials that are recommended in this book and in others written by Emilie Barnes. You may obtain a price list and seminar information by sending your request and a stamped, self-addressed business envelope to:

More Hours In My Day
2838 Rumsey Drive
Riverside, CA 92506

———— ♥ ————

Introduction

I really didn't know or care I was Jewish until I was 11 years old. Yes, I went to Sabbath school, synagogue, and high holy day services, but that eleventh year my father died. Mama had opened a small dress shop in Long Beach, California, and we lived in three little rooms behind that shop. With no other source of income, it was a way of putting food on the table during my father's two-year illness.

Mama was a caring Jewish mother who tried to keep her nest cozy, warm, and together. My Jewishness became real to me at that time and so did the fact that my mama needed a lot of support and help being a single working parent. My complete story can be read in our book *Growing A Great Marriage* (Harvest House Publishers).

I remember my mother always making our little place give a welcome feeling of love and friendship. Many times customers would tell their hurt and troubles to Mama and she would take them into our one room which served as a living room by day and a bedroom by night. Quickly a fresh cloth was slipped on the table, a candle lit, fresh flowers set out when available, and the teapot heated. Simple, yes, but oh so friendly. My job was to watch the store and take care of any customers while Mama listened to the woes of these women. Caring—you bet!—and it was learned by me through watching Mama. Today, I find myself doing the same things. It sure feels good.

Every day we have opportunities to care for our families, friends, neighbors, business associates—caring through organization, celebrating holidays and traditions, and on and on!

In the chapters that follow I want to share with you the

importance of little things (as well as bigger things) we can do to create caring in our lives.

Many "More Hours in My Day" women (women who have attended and grown through our seminars) will be sharing in this book practical ways of caring that are working for them.

This is a book of love and encouragement filled with tools, ideas, hints, and practical ways to care. As our example, we have the ultimate gift of caring: when God gave us His very own Son, Jesus Christ, as Messiah and Lord Immanuel—God Almighty.

Luke 10:38-42 (TLB) says,

As Jesus and the disciples continued on their way to Jerusalem they came to a village where a woman named Martha welcomed them into her home. Her sister Mary sat on the floor, listening to Jesus as he talked. But Martha was the jittery type, and was worrying over the big dinner she was preparing. She came to Jesus and said, "Sir, doesn't it seem unfair to you that my sister just sits here while I do all the work? Tell her to come and help me." But the Lord said to her, "Martha, dear friend, you are so upset over all these details! There is really only one thing worth being concerned about. Mary has discovered it—and I won't take it away from her!"

This truly is the dilemma of today's woman. I've been more like Martha than like Mary—I desire to be like Mary, but my Martha side keeps getting in the way. Is Mary the better woman? The Lord gave her the praise, yet if we were 100 percent like Mary, nothing would get done. Dorothy Main of Boger, Texas shares with us and gives evidence of that age-old dilemma:

My Martha Side

My house is a tyrant, demanding each hour. Imperiously ordering: "Sweep, mop and scour! Do the dishes, the laundry, then iron, dust and cook! And there's mending to do if you'll just take a look. Now, Martha, get busy and don't waste a minute; dirt is a sin, and you're wallowing in it!"

My Mary Side

My housework can wait... there's a friend I must see, who's lonely and frightened, she's looking for me. Then I'll tidy up quickly and hurry to hear that fine missionary we support every year. Home again, "Father, thank You, please help me to care for the hungry and homeless who live in despair."

Mary-Martha-Me

Martha nags me to keep my house spotless each day; and Mary says gently, "I need time to pray." Martha's concerned with "what neighbors might think if they dropped in and found dishes stacked in the sink." While Mary chides, "Selfish! I think it's a crime if you don't share with others your talents and time."

My Prayer

Oh God, in compassion, so order my days that Mary might serve Thee and Martha may praise Thee.

1 | *Caring for God*

———— ♥ ————

And I pray that Christ will be more and more at home in your hearts, living within you as you trust in him. May your roots go down deep into the soil of God's marvelous love; and may you be able to feel and understand as all God's children should, how long, how wide, how deep, and how high his love really is (Ephesians 3:17,18 TLB).

IT'S NOT USUAL THAT we would be home on a Friday evening, but we were on the night of June 23. We were to be conducting a marriage seminar in our home the next morning. We had everything organized and ready for the couples to arrive for the 9:00 A.M. first session. Bob and I were in the kitchen popping popcorn when the phone rang. I remember checking my watch, thinking who would be calling at this late time of 9:30 P.M. to get directions for tomorrow.

After Bob's first few words, I knew something serious had happened. Our dear friends of 20 years were calling for care, help, support, and prayers. Their son, Jimmy, had been in a terrible car accident on a street near our home— Victoria Avenue—and had hit a palm tree. That's all it took for Bob to say we would be right there.

We met Jim and Barbara DeLorenzo the first year we moved to Riverside. Jimmy was about 8 years old. They were new Christians and God truly bonded our hearts and friendship almost immediately. Over the years our families have experienced many memorable times. We still call Jim Jr. "Jimmy"; it's a habit, I guess.

But at that moment all we could think of was how dangerous Victoria Avenue is, with palm trees lining both sides and also in a row down the middle. The years our children were in high school, eight students died due to palm-tree accidents. But this couldn't be happening to Jimmy. He was an excellent driver, his dad had been into car safety, race meets, and rebuilding cars all his life. Jimmy knew very well the danger of Victoria Avenue and how to handle cars in dangerous situations. As we drove to the hospital, all we could do was pray and ask God to spare this child. The first words that came from Big Jim's mouth when they met us in emergency was "Jimmy wasn't driving and the two young men are alive."

The car was going 65 mph as it lost control on a curve and crashed into a palm tree and literally wrapped itself around the tree. The pictures later showed that only a miracle of God could explain their lives being spared. The metal "jaws of life" were used to cut these young men out of the car. Drugs and alcohol were immediately ruled out. If you've ever experienced an emergency room, you know the trauma, pain, and critical timing that is necessary—not to mention the emotional trauma of the loved ones involved. God truly puts caring people in those emergency rooms— no doubt about it.

Jim and Bob stayed with Jimmy and the doctors as they stitched up his lacerated head, eyes, and hands. Later, plastic surgery and more repairs were needed, but both young men survived. Barbara and I prayed. Rather, I prayed as she cried and shook from shock herself. We knew it was in God's hands. We also knew of other parents who weren't so lucky and had lost their sons and daughters through similar accidents.

Jimmy is okay today; however, only after plastic surgery, a shaved head, hundreds of stitches, and a plastic pin in his eye socket.

As Barbara and Jim reflect on the experience, they see what a precious time of love and friendship occurred. The bond we felt with them and them with us will always be there. As Barb says, "It's beyond words, the changes we've made with priorities in our life. The results have been a closer prayer life within the family and such growth of fellowship with God and friends, not to even mention the times we've had with our son and his recovery." Their roots of faith in God's love and protection have deepened and they do realize how wide, how high, and how deep God's love really is.

When we find ourselves in emergency situations, we realize only God is the one in control. May we never forget that!

Trusting God in Our Trials

I was doing a holiday seminar at Victoria Community Church (our church home) in Riverside, California. The church was filled with excited women (almost 800) eager to listen, learn, enjoy, and experience the day. Many of the MOPS (Mothers of Preschoolers) women had worked hard as a committee to make the event very festive and special for a relaxing Saturday seminar.

The day was to be videotaped for future use so women all over the country who couldn't come in person could gain the joy of this special day. (Video now available. See page 6.) The first half was going strong and the women were quiet and still, so eager to grasp every idea and word, when a little toddler began to walk up and down the aisle. This little one had been squeaking on and off, but not to this extent. In my thoughts I asked, "Where are the hostesses?

Where is a MOPS mom to help quiet this situation?" All I could think of was the distraction and the video picking up the noise. No one was to be seen. All the gals were busy preparing the lunches to be set out for the women.

Immediately as I continued speaking, trying not to lose my train of thought, I prayed in my mind, "Lord, please somehow quiet this child." Little cutie toddler kept up his fun up and down the aisle, and his mom didn't seem to think anything was wrong with it. No one was in sight to quietly go to her. "But the video will be ruined," I thought. There were seminar women who were paying sitters in order to have a special day out. As I continued to speak, my prayer continued that the Lord would stop the confusion and noise. To me, this time seemed like hours when in reality it was probably only a few minutes.

From absolutely nowhere, my Bob popped out—he was supposed to be in the gymnasium manning our book table and helping with the crafts and lunch preparations. He never comes into the seminar area at this time, but there he was. God heard my prayer and prompted Bob to check the sanctuary. He immediately and quietly asked the mom with the toddler to step into the cry room where she could see all and hear all. Thank you, Lord, for being interested in a speaker's prayer for silent babies. Thank You, God, for a husband who cares enough about God to listen to His voice.

Matthew 6:33 has been our life verse together: "But seek first His kingdom and His righteousness; and all these things shall be added to you."

A Commitment to Prayer

I had the opportunity once to host a radio talk show, "Great Tapes," in Southern California. Helen Fabin, a friend and host of this show, has been so supportive of our ministry. In fact, her husband, Paul, and his company did all our taping for our holiday video. Helen suggested I have a guest on the radio show that day and play a tape. The one name that came to my mind was Becky Tirabassi, a young woman I met through Florence Littauer's Christian Leaders and Speakers Seminars (CLASS). Becky has a great testimony and super ministry, especially with high school students. Her high school years were spent as an alcoholic. God touched her life. She married a special young man in Christian service and they now have a son. At one point in Becky's early Christian walk, she was convicted by God to spend one hour a day with the Lord in prayer. In today's busy world with many commitments, one hour a day for the rest of your life is quite a decision. That day my heart was touched by her deep love for the Lord, and so were the hearts of many listeners. I've not personally given that kind of a commitment of time to prayer in one sitting, but let me share what is working presently for me.

For the past five years my goal has been to walk 2-3 miles daily. It takes me about 30 to 40 minutes. Funny, isn't it, how we will find time to do an aerobics class, work out, run, walk, or other activities but not dedicate time for prayer. My time is well-planned each day and spent in my office preparing for seminars and speaking—not to mention letters to be answered, phone calls to make, and the keeping of our home. One of my encouraging messages to women is to teach yourself to do at least two things at a time. My quiet time begins early each day with Scripture reading for about 5-10 minutes. I then flip in my prayer notebook to the day of the week and review those whom I remember in prayer that day. My prayer organization works so well for me and is such an easy way of seeking first the kingdom of God. I'll share that with you at the end of the chapter. After my review of names and requests, off I go for my 30-minute walk. As I begin to walk, I begin to adore God and worship Him. Sometimes I sing a few songs, look around at the mountains, trees, bushes, and sky, and marvel at what He has given us. I've found myself raising my hands in the air to worship and praise Him for the opportunity He gives me to reach and touch women's lives. I then confess to Him my failures, inadequacies, and other areas of my life that I need to give to Him. From there I thank the Lord for His mighty forgiveness, His hands that always surround us with His love, the way He carries us when we are weak and tired, overwhelmed, downhearted, suffering, sick, in sorrow and shame. I'm just thankful always for the abundance we have. I'm thankful to you women who are reading this book right now, that you possess a teachable spirit with positive attitudes and are looking up for God's glory and direction instead of down for Satan's doom. By now I'm about halfway through my walk and ready to make my turn toward home to rejoice in His love and give my requests to God. I ask the Lord to bring to my mind and heart those I reviewed earlier in my prayer notebook for that specific day of the week, and the rest of my walk is spent praying for those dear requests. Much of this book has been inspired and prayed for as I walk daily.

As I reflected on my caring to spend time with Jesus, I realized I was committed to almost one hour daily. I got excited about this. God had convicted me as He had Becky Tirabassi, only in a different way. Here is how to set up your own personal prayer notebook. Some sample pages are at the end of this chapter. (To order a prayer notebook see page 6.)

Developing Your Prayer Notebook

Devote yourselves to prayer, keeping alert
in it with an attitude of thanksgiving.
(Colossians 4:2)

Items Needed:

1 three-ring binder (8½″ x 5½″ recommended)
1 set of "label-your-own" tabs
100 sheets of lined paper that fits into the binder for prayer requests, sermon outlines, notes, etc.

1. Divide prayer request sheets behind tabs labeled "Monday–Saturday."

2. Put sermon notes behind Sunday tab or Saturday tab (depending upon your day of worship).

3. Your last two tabs are for miscellaneous sections you can label yourself. Suggestions: goals; Bible study notes; daily Bible reading; personal prayer; favorite Scriptures; Scriptures memorized; names, addresses, phone numbers.

4. You are now ready to make a list of prayer requests:

   • *Family:* immediate and extended

   • *Personal:* between you and God

   • *Finances:* budget

   • *Illness*

   • *Career* and job-related

   • *Church:* pastor, staff, youth, etc.

   • *Missions:* missionaries; home; world ministries: Wycliffe, Mission Fellowship, Youth for Christ, Young Life, Campus Crusade for Christ, Inter-Varsity, Navigators, Billy Graham, Focus on the Family, 700 Club, "More Hours in My Day"

   • *Government:* local, state, national

   • *Schools:* preschool to college, etc.

5. Divide prayer request topics into each day of the week leaving Sunday tab (or day of Sabbath) for sermon notes/outlines. Your sections may look like this:

   Monday—*Family* (use one page for each member): Bob, Brad, Jenny, Craig, etc.

   Tuesday—*Church:* Senior pastor and family, youth, music, etc.

Wednesday—*Personal:* Organization: meal planning, home, weaknesses becoming strengths, relationships, goal setting, etc.

Thursday—*Finances:* Home, children, credit cards, overextending, retirement, investments, major purchases, auto/home/furniture.

Friday—*Illness:* Great Grandma Gertie—hip, Aunt Barbara—lupus, special friend Bill—glaucoma

Saturday/Sunday—*Government/Schools:* President of the United States, state and city leaders, day-care centers, colleges, etc.

Saturday/Sunday—*Sermon Notes/Outlines*

------------ ♥ ------------

But when you pray, go away by yourself, all alone, and shut the door behind you and pray to your Father secretly, and your Father, who knows your secrets, will reward you" (Matthew 6:6 TLB).

Ask God now to show you how you can seek first His kingdom and spend time in prayer daily with Jesus. It may not be as Becky or I do; it will be your own special appointment with God.

Prayer Basket

One last idea that works well for me is my prayer basket. In a basket will go the following tools for your appointment with God:

1. Prayer notebook
2. Pen
3. Bible
4. Tissue for tears

5. A small bunch of fresh or silk flowers to remind you of God's fragrance of love to us and of His Spirit who will permeate our hearts to overflow into the hearts of others.

6. A few cheery note cards so you can write a note of encouragement.

Your basket is ready at all times with the organizational materials you need for those special meetings with Jesus. Jesus went to the mountaintop to pray. My mountaintop is the walk along Gage Canal in Riverside, California. Yours may be the closet, bathroom, kitchen table, bedroom, yard, rocker, car, a bench in the park on a lunch break, or your office at work. But wherever it may be, let it be so your roots may go down deep into the soil of God's marvelous love. He loves you so much that He died for you and gave His life that you might receive eternal life as you receive and believe in Him.

> For God so loved the world, that He gave His only begotten Son, that whoever believes in Him should not perish, but have eternal life. For God did not send the son into the world to judge the world, but that the world should be saved through Him (John 3:16,17).

These verses touched my heart when as a young 16-year-old Jewish girl I heard about God's beautiful plan. My Bob loved and cared for my eternal soul and life. He shared his love with me for God the Father, God the Son, and God the Holy Spirit. During my sixteenth year I had an eternal decision to make. I did love God; I went to Hebrew school and was confirmed in the synagogue. But when Bob shared with me about Jesus as Messiah, he really made it clear to me that I did have a need in my heart that only Christ could fill. As I opened my heart to Jesus, the emptiness disappeared. I felt the comfort of His Spirit and felt for the first time in my life that I would never be alone. I was hungry for

God's Word. Bob was excited to share with me and teach me, and I was excited to learn.

At 17, I became Mrs. Bob Barnes. Many said it would never last. I knew in my heart it could work as long as we both had the common goal of seeking first the kingdom of God. Bob was teaching school and, to be honest, I was only four years older than his students. In fact, during my senior year in high school Bob signed my report cards.

Remembering to Pray

At 20, our Jenny was born and at 21 we had five children under the age of five. We took in my brother's three children when their mother abandoned them, and our Brad came along shortly thereafter. I don't think I could have possibly made it had I not cared about God. I'm still growing and learning. It has taken me 35 years of growth and I'm not finished yet, nor is God finished with me yet.

When he was 29 years old, our son Brad became very ill—the worst I had ever seen him. He had canker sores throughout his mouth, throat, and into the esophagus and stomach. He couldn't swallow, his temperature went up to 104 degrees, and he became dehydrated. We had no idea what was wrong. He broke out with a red rash all over his body which we thought was an allergic reaction to the medication the doctor was giving him. As I held him I prayed that our loving, caring God would touch his body and remove his sickness. Brad didn't get any better; in fact, he seemed to get worse. I prayed again, "But God, You promised You would heal the sick. Our son is critically ill." That afternoon Bob loaded Brad into our car and took him to Dr. Merrihew, who immediately diagnosed him with the red measles. Brad was born in 1960 and it wasn't until 1962 that the vaccine was given. Somehow our children were never given the prevention vaccine. It's been known for adults to die with the measles, so I called our church and asked for prayer. At once the prayer chain began praying for Brad.

One woman called three women who each called three women until over 40 people were lifting Brad up to the Lord for healing. The comfort it gave Brad to know that others whom he didn't even know were praying for him was unbelievable. My elderly Jewish auntie even said she would pray for him. When I told her about the prayer chain of women she said, "What's that?" Tears came to her eyes as I explained it and she said, "I'll pray, too." Now, that was a miracle! But then that's God's special business, isn't it, ministering His Spirit to others? At 86, she just may become a believer yet. As Brad lay so ill, he proposed to the young woman he loved, and in July they were married. Yes, God healed Brad and also used his illness in ways we will never know on earth, but melodies of Jesus' touch will be sung in heaven.

I'm sure many of you readers have experienced far greater crises. It is times like these that our only source of peace comes from those who care enough to pray for us when we just can't. A card, a note, a phone call says we care and will pray. These "cares" say volumes to those who hurt.

May I never forget to say thank-you to those who care and love God, who pray for others in a world of busyness. And may I never forget where our source of strength, peace, joy, and healing is. "Thank You, Jesus, that You cared for this little Jewish girl. Touch her heart for You, that she might serve and love You more each day of her life, and may she never forget to pray." Matthew 6:33 (KJV) says, "Seek first His kingdom and His righteousness; and all these things shall be added to you." This verse will always be a strength in our home.

———— ♥ ————

*Love is something
you do.*

PRAYER REQUESTS

Date	Request	Scripture	Update/Answer	Date
7/1	Evelyn's mother's surgery		all's well	7/3
7/1	Kevin's graduation		with honors	7/1
7/3	the Field's baby		much better	7/6
7/5	Grandma's hospital stay		improving released	7/8 7/10
7/7	Jennifer's tooth		pulled	7/9
7/8	Brad's Escrow	Phil. 4:19	closed	7/9
7/9	Craig's home loan	Matt. 6:8	reapplied approved	7/12 7/25
7/12	Aunt Gladys' funeral		great to be a Christian	7/12
7/20	Pastor Foor is sick		preached on Sunday	7/24
7/21	Inter-varsity committee			
7/23	Bevan's fever		down to normal	7/25
7/25	Christine's 1st date		she was so pretty	7/27
7/28	Chad's summer league tryout		he made the team	7/29
7/30	Phil Jackson's surgery		not doing well	

SERMON NOTES

Date: 7/8/90   **Speaker:** Pastor Don Foor
Title: Our response to what's inside our
Text: Psalm 51:10-12,   hearts
              Mark 7:6-7

I. What is most important?
   A. What seems most important
      to man:
      1. style - how we worship
      2. ritual & ceremony
      3. traditions
   These are not important to God.

   B. What God says is most important
      to Him:
      1. heart
      2. mind
      3. spirit

II. Take a look at our hearts
   A. We need God's help in our
      hearts.   Ps. 51:10-12
   B. We need God's help in seeing
      the truth of our hearts.
                    Ps. 139:23-24
   C. We need to keep our hearts
      close to God. Mark 7:6-7

Lord, your faith alone will I seek.

Lord, my heart waits for you.

Lord, my heart follows after you.

Subject Women's Ministry

1/4/90 – 1st committee meeting.
We will be hosting the 6th
Annual Retreat at
Arrowhead Springs. Campus
Crusade – Patsy Claremont
Speaking.

2/15/90 – Reports from the following
chairpersons:
Decorations
Invitations
Publicity
Food
Transportation
All's on schedule

3/13/90 – Opened in prayer
All committees reported
Specific prayer for
speaker and women
attending.
Next meeting 4/17 @ 9:00am

2 | *Things Happen When Women Care for Themselves*

—————— ♥ ——————

You shall love the Lord your God with all your heart, and with all your soul, and with all your mind. . . . You shall love your neighbor as yourself (Matthew 22:37-39).

GOD GAVE THE ABOVE verses of Scripture originally in Deuteronomy 6:4-9 to the Jewish nation as part of their Shema which became Judaism's basic confession of faith. According to rabbinic law, this passage was to be recited every morning and night. This passage stresses the uniqueness of God, precludes the worship of other gods, and demands a total love commitment.

In Matthew 22 Jesus was asked, "Teacher, which is the great commandment in the Law?" He gave two commandments which stress three loves: the love of God, the love of self, and the love of your neighbor. In our culture we are taught to love God and we know we are to be kind and love our neighbors, but somehow we have a difficult time knowing how to love ourselves. The church has taught that we are not to dwell too long on our personal selves and that we are to give to others. I have found many women who do not know how to love themselves. As women we always seem to be giving so much to others in our family that there is no time left for us.

As a young woman and a new bride, then as a new mother, I was always tired. I had no energy left over for me, and we most certainly didn't have enough money left over from our budget to give me anything. So what did I do for myself? Not very much. After studying this passage of Scripture, I was challenged to study the subject of personal worth—not an overemphasis on self, but a balanced and moderate approach that would let me grow as an individual. I knew if God was going to make me a complete and functioning person in the body of Christ I had to develop a wholesome approach to this area of caring for myself.

As I began to look about me, I found women who had a mistrust of themselves and had begun to withhold love and self-acceptance—women who had no idea that God had a plan for their life, and whose lives reflected fear, guilt, and mistrust of other people.

In the 1980's awareness of this whole topic of the dysfunctional family let us realize that most of us come from a family with some sort of abnormality. We begin to manifest those early childhood fears, guilt, and mistrust of others because we don't want to be hurt, scared, or disappointed again. Along with these manifestations, Satan makes us believe that we are totally unworthy as persons, and certainly not worthy to spend any extra time or money on.

As I looked around in my association with women at church, support groups, and home Bible studies, I found women who did not understand that God had given them, at birth, certain divine dignity which could make it possible for them to love themselves, and realize they are worthy of love. Women would relate to their friends either positively or negatively depending how well they understood this principle.

I can remember that one Friday morning while we were studying a marriage book Amy spoke up and said that she didn't take care of her personal self because her father had told her at a young age that pretty girls with good clothes and a nice figure stood a better chance of being molested by older boys and men as they grew up. At that time Amy decided she would not let herself be molested by an older man, so she began to gain weight, wear sloppy clothes, and certainly not look good in a bathing suit. She even remarked that her husband liked her this way because then other men didn't try to flirt with her. He was safe from any competition, and he liked that.

Over the next several months in our weekly study, I began to share how this fear was put there by Satan and not by God. I took extra time encouraging her to be all that God had for her. We looked at her eating habits and why she chose certain foods. After a while she began to seek professional counseling to understand what she was hiding behind. Today if you would see Amy you would see a fine young lady who has a totally new image and who shares with other women in full confidence that she is worthy of caring for herself. Because of Amy's self-appraisal, her husband has also joined a support group at church and has lessened his fears from his own insecurities.

What is anger? What is hatred? It is really fear. And what is fear? It is a feeling of being threatened, a deep feeling of insecurity. And what causes that feeling of insecurity? It is a lack of confidence in our ability to cope with threatening situations. And lack of self-confidence is the result of too low a value of yourself—you aren't able to love yourself because of what you think you are!

R.C. Sproul in one of his tapes says that "lack of faith" is a "lack of trust" that God is capable of doing what He has promised He will do.

It takes a lot of faith to love. Non-self-loving persons do not dare to love. They are afraid they'll be spurned or rejected. Why do they have that fear? Because they do not trust themselves or rate themselves high enough to believe they'll be loved. And why do they fear rejection? Because rejection will only put salt in the wounds, proving again to the person that they aren't worthy.

In Genesis 1:26,27 it says,

> Then God said, "Let Us make man in Our image, according to Our likeness...." And God

created man in His own image, in the image of
God He created him; male and female He created
them.

In verse 31 the Scripture says, "God saw all that He had
made, and behold, it was very good." We were spiritually
designed to enjoy the honor that befits a prince of heaven.
There is a basic need to recognize the dignity of the human
being to be a child of God.

Recently George Gallup, Jr., of the Gallup organization
released the findings of a poll his organization conducted
on the self-esteem of the American public. The poll con-
clusively demonstrated that people with a strong sense of
caring for themselves demonstrate the following qualities:

1. They have a high moral and ethical sensitivity.
2. They have a strong sense of family.
3. They are far more successful in interpersonal relationships.
4. Their perspective of success is viewed in terms of
   interpersonal relationships, not in crass mate-
   rialistic terms.
5. They're far more productive on the job.
6. They are far lower in incidents of chemical addic-
   tions. (In view of the fact that current research
   studies show that 80 percent of all suicides are
   related to alcohol and drug addiction, this becomes
   terribly significant.)
7. They are more likely to get involved in social and
   political activities in their community.
8. They are far more generous to charitable insti-
   tutions and give far more generously to relief
   causes.[1]

These are positive qualities that each of us want as
contributing members of our family, church, community,

and society. This same poll reflected that 35 percent of Protestants who were polled did have a strong love of themselves. The majority of our churches struggle in implementing the three loves of Deuteronomy and Matthew. We are challenged to teach that people who view God as a personal, loving, and forgiving Being, and relate to Him in such a personal way, do develop a strong, healthy sense of self-worth. Make sure you are in a church that teaches these aspects of the gospel.

Paul teaches in Philippians 4:13 that, "I can do all things through Him who strengthens me." Using this principle we can realize that Christ gives us the inner strength to care for ourselves. We must choose to love ourselves. There are many forces that say self-love is evil and wrong, but I want to encourage you to take time for yourself each day. Time for yourself gives you time to reflect on renewal of your mind, body, and spirit. Not only will you be rewarded, but so will those who come in contact with you daily.

Manifestations of the Three Loves

Paul in his writing to the church at Ephesus includes a section of Scripture to the believers on their relationship to the Holy Spirit. Beginning in Ephesians 5:18 we learn that we are to be satisfied with self, God, and others:

> And do not get drunk with wine, for that is dissipation, but be filled with the Spirit, speaking to one another in psalms and hymns and spiritual songs, singing and making melody with your heart to the Lord (verses 18,19).

If we are satisfied with ourselves, Paul teaches us to manifest it in speaking and singing words of joy. Our lives will be ones of joy, praise, and excitement. They will reflect positive thoughts, ideas, and praises to God. What a great test to see where our personal satisfaction is! Are we known as a person who is fun to be around, or are we one who people avoid? God wants us to be satisfied with ourselves and reflect the joy of the Lord in our soul, mind, and spirit.

Paul continues in verse 20, "Always giving thanks for all things in the name of our Lord Jesus Christ to God, even the Father" (NASB). This verse shows *our satisfaction with God.* If we are satisfied, we find ourselves giving thanks for all things. We have an appreciative heart for all that goes on around us. The positive words flow from our lips not only toward ourselves but unto God. Always have a thankful heart.

Our third satisfaction is with other people, and in verse 21 Paul teaches, "And be subject to one another in the fear of Christ." As women, we find that when we love God and ourselves, we become equipped to be submissive one to another. These words "subject" and/or "submissive" have taken a beating in today's culture, but in essence they are telling us to be satisfied with other people to the point that we are willing to step aside in our personal relationships in a Christian household. The subjection is to be mutual and based on reverence for God. It is humanly impossible to be subject one to another by human desire. It is possible only when we mutually do it one to another out of respect for God.

This passage of Scripture truly gives us guidelines for being satisfied with God, with ourselves, and with others.

As I have taught this concept over the years, I have used a diagram that has been a good teaching tool. It is:

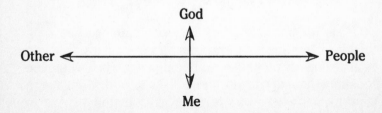

As you can see from the above diagram, we have vertical and horizontal relationships. The vertical relationship is between God and me and the horizontal relationship is between myself and other people. I find that when God and I have the proper relationship, my relationship with others falls into proper alignment. If I have dissatisfaction with myself and others, I realize that I am not responding to God properly. Over the years, God has taught me to put first things first: to love God, to love self, and to love others.

Sharpen the Saw

Steven R. Covey in his book *The Seven Habits of Highly Effective People* tells a story that reflects the need for renewal and reawakening in our lives.

> Suppose you come upon a man in the woods feverishly sawing down a tree.
>
> "You look exhausted!" you exclaim. "How long have you been at it?"
>
> "Over five hours," he replies, "and I'm beat. This is hard."
>
> "Maybe you could take a break for a few minutes and sharpen that saw. Then the work would go faster."
>
> "No time," the man says emphatically. "I'm too busy sawing."
>
> To sharpen the saw means renewing ourselves in all four aspects of our natures:
>
> *Physical*—exercise, nutrition, stress management;
>
> *Mental*—reading, thinking, planning, writing;
>
> *Social/Emotional*—service, empathy, security;
>
> *Spiritual*—spiritual reading, study, and meditation.
>
> To exercise in all these necessary dimensions, we must be proactive. No one can do it for us or make it urgent for us. We must do it for ourselves.[2]

If we are to stay on top of the pile rather than under the pile we must take time to smell the roses and to sharpen the saws of our lives. As I speak in front of various groups, I find many women who are defeated and burned out from their roles in life. Many women express to me, "If I only had time for myself, I would!"

Below I have given you several ideas that will help you care for yourself.

Physical:

- Get a professional massage, sauna, and steam bath.
- Have your hair and nails done.
- Exercise regularly by walking, jogging, aerobics, jazz-ercise, etc.
- Read a book on nutrition and begin to change your eating habits. My suggestion is *Eating Right* (Harvest House Publishers).
- Take a stress management class.
- Take a quiet bubble bath by candlelight.
- Have a pedicure done.
- Take a stroll on the beach, by the lake, or along a mountain trail.
- Plant a flower and/or vegetable garden.
- Walk or run in the rain.

Mental:

- Listen to good music.
- Read a good magazine or book.
- Retreat to a spot for a quiet time of meditating and reflecting.
- Spend time alone.
- Write a poem.

- Write a letter to an old friend.
- Plan your next three months' goals.
- Enroll in a self-help class at your local college.
- Think of possible changes in your life.
- Say "no" to good things and save your "yeses" for the best things.
- List everything for which you are thankful.
- Memorize a poem.
- Learn to play an instrument.
- Go to the beach and listen to the waves.
- Reach back to joyful times as a child and think about them.

Social/Emotional:

- Have a good cry.
- Have breakfast or lunch with a friend.
- Go to the mall and people-watch.
- Have a friend over for tea or coffee.
- Spend a day doing anything you want.
- Spend a weekend with your husband in a quiet setting—just to regroup.
- Visit a friend.
- Develop friendships with new people.
- Buy a bouquet of flowers for yourself.
- Donate time to a school, hospital, or church.
- Volunteer to collect money for United Way, the Cancer Society, or the Heart Association.
- Serve a friend in need.

Spiritual:

- Read the Psalms.
- Meditate on Scripture.
- Read a spiritual book that you have had lying on your kitchen table for some time.
- Write your worries in the sand at the beach.
- Join a women's Bible study.
- Visit someone at the hospital or nursing home.
- Give of yourself.
- Examine your motives (are they self-serving or serving others?).
- Listen to good Christian music.

Make up your own list of ideas under each of the headings. Learn to care for yourself. God felt it was such a valuable concept that He stated it as one of the two great commandments. Jesus went on to say that on these two commandments depend the whole law and prophets.

Yes, it's okay to care for yourself because Jesus said it was. Let's plan time in each of our days to *care for ourselves*.

Give yourself an opportunity to be and do something different. We are to become positive in all that we do.

Believe What God Believes About You

We as women are to believe that we have value and we are worthy of giving time and money to ourselves. The main step we must take in developing this process is to accept what our heavenly Father believes about us. Christian psychologist Dr. Dick Dickerson has written a paraphrase of 1 Corinthians 13 which beautifully summarizes how God looks at us. Read this passage aloud to yourself each morning and evening for the next 30 days, then evaluate how your feelings about yourself have changed:

Because God loves me, He is slow to lose patience with me.

Because God loves me, He takes the circumstances of my life and uses them in a constructive way for my growth.

Because God loves me, He does not treat me as an object to be possessed and manipulated.

Because God loves me, He has no need to impress me with how great and powerful He is because He is God. Nor does He belittle me as His child in order to show me how important He is.

Because God loves me, He is for me. He wants me to mature and develop in His love.

Because God loves me, He does not send down His wrath on every little mistake I make, of which there are many.

Because God loves me, He does not keep score of all my sins and then beat me over the head with them whenever He gets a chance.

Because God loves me, He is deeply grieved when I do not walk in the ways that please Him because He sees this as evidence that I don't trust Him and love Him as I should.

Because God loves me, He rejoices when I experience His power and strength and stand up under the pressure of life for His name's sake.

Because God loves me, He keeps working patiently with me even when I feel like giving up and can't see why He doesn't give up with me too.

Because God loves me, He keeps on trusting me when at times I don't even trust myself.

> Because God loves me, He never says there is no hope for me, rather, He patiently works with me, loves me and disciplines me in such a way that it is hard for me to understand the depth of His concern for me.
>
> Because God loves me, He never forsakes me even though many of my friends might.[3]

"Please be patient with me. God isn't finished with me yet." That is certainly true! As we look at a particular area in our lives, we can be tempted to break into tears of discouragement because we feel so defeated. But God is still working in our lives and will never give up on us.

God has put into each of our lives a void that cannot be filled by the world. We may leave God or put Him on hold, but He is always there, patiently waiting for us to run our race and become fatigued in the process, and then to turn back to Him.

Recently I got a letter from a lady who shares her struggle with life and had the courage to do something to rekindle that first love for God.

———————— ♥ ————————

Dear Bob and Emilie,

Just closed the last page in your book *Growing a Great Marriage*. I rejoice and thank you for writing such a wonderful, heartfelt book. I only wish I had had your kind of marriage from the beginning, but I was not a Christian then and didn't know the full impact of what a Christian marriage could be.

I am 46 years old, been married four times, and have five children and six grandchildren. The important part of all of this is I accepted the Lord in 1972 with my third husband. He just couldn't handle the Christian life, and so he left in 1974. But I continued to stay with my church, worked for a

Christian ministry, and kept my children in a church atmosphere as much as possible. But in 1983 I became restless and left my church and work and married a Marine 20 years younger than I. We have been together for eight years, longer than any of my other marriages, and I am committed to staying with this person for life.

When I left everything in 1983, I had no idea of what I was really leaving behind: a great church, good Christian fellowship, and dear, dear friends. What an unrestful time we experience when we are out of Christian fellowship. I believe now that I have been dying a slow death because of not being in fellowship with my Jesus and Lord.

I will joyously try to share your book with three of my daughters. All my children know Christ as their Savior, but none are walking with Him.

Well, you two, thank you for such a wonderful, honest book. I venture to say I will read it more than once.

By the way, three weeks ago I started attending Fallbrook Presbyterian Church—first time in eight years. Also went to a women's Bible study and could have listened for hours.

Love in Christ,

Linda Street
Southern California

——————— ♥ ———————

As you become secure in God's love, you will discover that you need not surrender your caring for yourself to the opinions and judgments of others. GOD IS FOR YOU!

——————— ♥ ———————

*A woman must keep
her friendships
in constant repair.*

3 | *Caring for Singles*

————— ♥ —————

For I have learned to be content, whatever the circumstances (Philippians 4:11 NIV).

I AM A PRODUCT of a single working mother. As an 11-year-old girl, I saw my chef father, Otto, die of a massive heart attack and leave my dear mother, Irene, to raise me and my older brother, Eddie. Singleness was an abrupt, new, and unexpected dimension for Mama. Even though her father had been a tailor in New York City and she had been a seamstress in his store, she was not trained for a career or for running a business. Somehow she needed to launch upon a new challenge of making a living for herself and two young children. Taking advantage of her past skills, she (along with the help and encouragement of her sister, Syd) opened a small ladies' apparel store in Long Beach, California.

Little did I realize that the lessons I was going to learn in the next few years were to prove most valuable to me throughout life. What was the rare exception in those days has now become conventional for the 1990's. By the latest polls, a mother or father is missing in almost seven million households with children under 18. America has experienced a single-parent explosion. In just the last 40 years in America the single-parent phenomenon has gone from 4 million to over 20 million—an increase of almost 400 percent.

The impact on children has been great. In the mid 1980's over 13 million children under 18 lived with one parent, an increase of 66 percent in the last ten years. In nine out of ten cases the mother, usually divorced, is the custodial parent. Demographers expect that soon 44 percent of all children under 18 will be living with one parent. In our churches today we must begin to address this new dimension of God's body. For many years the church has been "couple and family" oriented. If we continue on that course, we will be excluding at least 50 percent of our church population. Not only will we be missing out on ministering to a large section of the adult population, but we will also be neglecting the children of these single parents.

Many churches throughout America are beginning to recognize this new group and have appointed a pastor to head up this ministry. This group does have some unique distinctions which must be addressed. For many years we have thought of the single mother and her particular needs; however, now we are beginning to realize that the single lifestyle is made up of:

- The single person who has never been married.
- Divorced mothers with custody.
- Divorced fathers with custody.
- Divorced parents without custody.
- The single, never-married parent.
- The single, widowed person.

The single life is full of problems: loneliness, relating to people, trusting others, sex, and fitting into today's church.

How does the single person deal with single living? There are three areas where we can wrestle with these problems and gain new truths: the Bible, the church, and within ourselves. God is faithful with His Word, and the Bible remains an organized and exciting pattern for life and living.

It might seem like the church is an obvious place to find the answer, yet many singles have had to ask, "Where do we fit in?" If the church is to help, singles must let the church minister to them, and contribute in whatever way they can to the church. Because the church today is geared to family life, singles find few ways to express their gifts and give service to the church. The married church needs the single person and the single person needs exposure to people of every lifestyle: the married, the single, the widowed, and the elderly. In Galatians 6:2 the writer shares that we are to bear one another's burdens and thus fulfill the law of Christ. Yes, we are to bear each other's burdens in order to be part of one another. Our church programs must be integrated with other ministries in order to meet the needs of the total body of Christ.

As God's people, the church has a heritage that is neither single nor married, but one of unity in Christ. The Christian's basic identity is in being a child of the God who created him and who is willing to create magnificent works in his life.

In talking with people in various forms of singleness, I find that the women state their number-one problem as being depression. Worry, self-concern, and a lowered standard of living are close behind. These concerns seem to directly affect their children. Moms feel that they are unable to provide childcare and other necessities for their children as they feel they should.

The few single fathers that I have talked to state that their concerns are different. The single father's number-one concern is that his child gets good care while Dad's at work. There are many resources which a parent has available: day-care centers (many are now housed in local churches), family (grandparents can be a great resource if they are willing, have good health, and live close by), professional babysitters, counseling services, neighbors, and friends. Each single parent must search out how to solve his or her unique problems.

As I look back to my youth, I can remember the positive attitude my mother had in being single. From life's experiences I can tell you that we chose happiness, good self-esteem, joy, and optimism each day. Parents pass on healthy or unhealthy attitudes to their children. How parents relate to their new single role will greatly affect how the children perceive their status in life.

I can remember my mom telling me a story that occurred when she was living as a young orphaned girl in New York City. After her parents died, she literally raised her younger brother and sisters. There were many days the family did not have enough food for each meal. Mama would boil a saucepan of water and add a rock to the water. After boiling it for a while she would add salt and pepper for flavor and dish out the liquid into a soup bowl for each of the children. A younger sister would ask, "What kind of soup tonight?" and Mama would gleefully reply, "Rock soup." Her brother knew better, but the attitude was one of appreciation for God's daily provision. They chose a good attitude.

Mothers, we set the thermostats in our homes. There will be days which are great where everything goes as planned, and there will be other days when we aren't sure why we got out of bed. Regardless of which day it is, we can be assured that God takes care of our daily needs.

"How thankful I am to Christ Jesus our Lord for choosing me as one of his messengers, and giving me the strength to be faithful to him" (1 Timothy 1:12 TLB). Andrew Murray states, "I have learned to place myself before God every day as a vessel to be filled with His Holy Spirit. He has filled me with the blessed assurance that He, as the everlasting God, has guaranteed His own work in me."[1]

Child psychologist David Elkind, author of *The Hurried Child*, says that single parents, crushed by the weight of sole responsibility, often force their children into the role of pseudoadult and confidant. He states that this might serve the parents' needs, but it is not clear that this is what the children need. Other authorities in this area state that the greatest problem with single parents is that the children are forced to grow up too fast, to behave as adults. Many children become overburdened by the passed-along pressures of the parents. At age 9 or 10, children simply can't be asked to give advice about the stock market, marriage, or divorce. The young child pushed into such an adult role always suffers later in life from lack of self-esteem. Small children just can't live up to such expectations (whether real or imagined).

There is much confusion among the experts, particularly when it comes to the effects of divorce on a child. There is one place where research does agree: The stronger and more positive the custodial parent, the less likely it is that the child will have problems adjusting to the single-parent household.

I recently received a letter from Mary in Florida, which helps validate this point.

Dear Emilie,

Thank you so very much for taking the time to write all of your books on organization and time management. They have been so refreshing to me as a young wife. I came from a divorced family and was raised by my father, since my mother suffered from lack of emotional stability. In the early beginning (when I was 12) he did not have any experience on how to cook, wash, and take care of the home, but his sister lived nearby and she was a big help to teach us both.

Dad was a real champion and had a great attitude toward his new role. He always had a smile on his face and heart. He never reflected to me that life had dealt him the wrong cards. I really love Dad because he loved me so very much. I consider your books to be a continuation of that learning process. May God richly bless you in your ministry.

Love, Mary

If the custodial parent is so battered by circumstances that he or she alarms the child's sense of well-being and distorts realities, the parent will have an anxious child with a skewed view of life. If the parent is able to make the child feel loved and secure in spite of adversity, the child will thrive.

In my seminars I try to give parents several ideas regarding this area of developing a sense of love in the family. The whole area of time management is so crucial during this phase of a person's life. If we can reduce the stresses and tensions of disorganization, we have eliminated a major cause of anxiety, frustration, and tears. A couple of techniques are described below.

The Memory Plate

In the early days of our country, mothers would have one unique plate that they reserved for special use by members of the family. When there was a birthday, wedding, anniversary, baptism, or dedication, Mom would bring out this plate and present it to the person who was being honored. With this plate came a special time for praise, recognition, songs, and even a short toast honoring the family member for his or her special day. That tradition has even been carried forward into the 1990's. There are many commercial memory plates on the market. Moms have told me they just take an ordinary plate (not one of your regular china plates) and designate that to be used among the family members.

The other night in San Diego a lady told me she uses this same idea and makes it available to her family on a random basis every two weeks. After the family goes to bed at night, she writes one of their names on the calendar hanging in the kitchen and the next morning the children rush to the calendar to see who is going to be honored.

The child chosen gets to pick a favorite meal for the evening. This mom was so excited about the results of the memory plate idea, and she expressed how thrilled the children were when it became their turn.

"I Was Caught Being Good" Stickers

Berg Christian Enterprises in Portland, Oregon, manufactures stickers with teddy bears on them that read: "I Was Caught Being Good." When we catch our children doing something good we are to praise them. So many mothers have shared what a great tool this has been in motivating their children to help around the home. Children must be made to realize that they contribute to their family. Without this awareness of contribution, they will feel that they aren't needed and the family can do just as well without them! These stickers really let children know they are recognized and appreciated for their contributions.

With our grandchildren we go one step further. After they have worn their stickers around the house and before they go back to their home, we have them place their used stickers on an 8½" x 11" sheet of paper. When they have ten stickers on a sheet, we redeem the sheet back for one dollar. Several moms with teenagers say it works for them, too, but they have had to increase the redemption value (this will depend upon your economic situation).

"I Love You Because..." Cards

A packet of 64 assorted colored cards come pre-printed with the words "I Love You Because..." You as a parent can write a personalized message to your child like, "Dear Christine, I love you because you always come to the breakfast table with a smile. Love, Mom."

What a great way to start the day. Insert a card under a pillow, by a toothbrush, under a glass of milk at the table, in a sack lunch, or even mail it to your child in a special envelope. So many warm feelings emerge from these warm thoughts.

During the holiday season I received the following letter from a lady who had attended one of my holiday seminars in Southern California.

> Dear Emilie,
>
> When I left your holiday seminar in Mission Viejo, I was so excited and encouraged for Thanksgiving Day to come because my family was going to be at our house this year for dinner. I really like your idea on using your "I Love You Because..." cards with each person writing something nice about the person on their left as they were seated at dinner. As we began to read what had been written I began to see tears appear in my family's eyes. Even the macho men who never show any softness were touched by words of kindness.
>
> That evening as I said prayers with my young children, each one liked the idea and wanted to know if we could do it again next year. My 7-year-old daughter, Suzie, commented that Aunt Joy said she loved me because I always gave her a kiss when we were together.
>
> I just want to encourage you to keep on doing what you and Bob are doing for our families. You both are a real model of inspiration and encouragement.
>
> In His Service,
>
> Betty Anne

Chore Charts

As children perceive their worth and value to the family based on how they feel about their contributions to their family, the chore charts really help them realize they are contributors and they are needed in order for the family to function properly. At a very young age (2½–3 years old) they can begin to be responsible for some areas in the home: personal hygiene, dusting their furniture (they may not always get it quite clean), picking up clothes, taking dirty clothes to the laundry area, helping set the table, cleaning dishes off the table (with two hands), etc. In the early years your chore charts can have simple pictures with a water-base marking pen for checking off the chore when completed, and then advance to a printed list on the refrigerator or bulletin board when the children are able to read. Whatever the ages of the children, they need a check-list to show how they are doing. You can also think up some type of reward system when they have completed all their chores for the week. Be sure to inspect each chore to make sure it is done satisfactorily.

I have a little saying that says: *It's not what you expect as much as what you inspect!*

All of these ideas help instill in your child a healthy attitude toward home. It will also make child-raising more fun for you as Mom. Positive energy is always more reward-ing than negative energy. It will do a lot toward reflecting the proper attitude from you to the children.

The Problem of Guilt

One of the major enemies of a positive attitude is guilt. Many single parents can't be positive about parenting because they feel they have done wrong to their children. The single parent should remember two things:

1) It's important to distinguish between psychologi-cal and theological guilt. All guilt feelings aren't because we have violated God's laws. Many times guilt comes from how we were raised by controlling parents or ex-partners.

2) We must know that the opposites of sin and guilt are grace and forgiveness. In Romans 5:20, Paul shares that the more we see of our sinfulness, the more we see God's abounding grace forgiving us.

Sin and guilt actually provide God with the opportunity to show how gracious and loving He is.

Our children will lay on guilt in our life and we have to be aware of the guilt game. It will set in if we are not sensitive to what is happening. The following story demonstrates "the working mother's guilt." It goes like this:

Hello, Mom? Is that you? I know you don't like me to phone you at work and all, but where's the Sweet 'n Low? Huh? Oh, it's for the firemen. No, everything's real okay now, Mom. Nothing to worry about. The firemen put out the fire right away. The fire? Oh, that was when I tried to make grilled cheese sandwiches and forgot to take the plastic off the cheese so it caught fire. I know that I was supposed to make peanut butter and jelly sandwiches. But I couldn't, Mom. Huh? No peanut butter, that's why.

Well, Mom, I have to give the firemen their Sweet 'n Low now, and then I'm going next door to Mrs. Jones' house.

Well, when she saw the firemen come she invited me over for soda. She said she didn't believe that mothers should be working all the time to pay the mortgage and that they should stay home until their kids went away to college, just like she did. Well, 'bye.[2]

Then there is "the latch-key guilt."

Well, Bobby, I had the hardware store put a little plastic ring with a different color on each key, see? So you can tell them apart. Now this key is for the lobby door, only don't ever let anyone in you don't know. Wait outside until one of our neighbors comes.

Now this key is for the top door lock—the orange key. And this one is for the bottom door lock. You know that's the one that sticks and sometimes you have to push the door in and kick it and then turn the key really hard to the left while kicking the door again. But that's easy to remember! I'm sure you'll have no trouble with it.

And then if you'll just remember to keep the keys on the string around your neck, and when you're home never open the door for anyone and never answer the telephone unless it's me, but I always ring three times first, so you'll know. Why, it'll go just fine, right?[3]

When single parents can begin to see the humor of the guilt games they play with themselves and other people, they can be sure they are beginning to rid themselves of guilt. A recent article in our local paper written to Ann Landers exhibits a good balance that all parents should have regarding their relationship with their children. It was entitled "Don't Expect Praise for Just Being Good."

Dear Ann Landers: This clipping is well-worn from years on the bulletin board. I am a teacher in Valdosta, GA, and it was here when I came. I don't know where it came from, but I believe it deserves a larger audience. Please print it. T.C.

Dear T.C.: It had a larger audience. It appeared in my column several years ago. Thank you for asking.

SORRY, NO MEDAL FOR YOU, KID

A teen-ager came up to me and said, "Gee, Good Adult, why aren't you proud of me? I've never been arrested and I'm a really good kid. It seems that nobody understands me."

You say nobody understands you and then you brag about how you resisted being a bandit, a dropout and menace to society. Also, you don't smoke dope or hit your teacher. You work after school and are a joy to your parents.

I do not go around robbing gas stations or shooting people, either. My reward is that I don't get thrown in jail. That is also your reward. You don't punch your teacher and I don't punch my boss. So you get an education and I get to keep my job. You don't hot rod your car and I don't hot rod mine. We both may live longer and that is a pretty nice reward isn't it?

You work after school. I work after work. We both get money, which is handy when you want to buy something. And don't forget that for many years I have been contributing part of my paycheck to build those schools you brag about not dropping out of.

Your reward for staying in school is an education that will help you get a better job, or maybe be a doctor or a lawyer. Education can help you live a fuller life and be a Good Adult. So stop looking for praise for doing what you are supposed to do. That's what you're here for.[4]

Singleness As a Choice

Not everyone chooses marriage, for the first time or even as an alternative after divorce. Recent statistics point out that 50 percent of first marriages fail, but 60 percent of second marriages fail. The warning we have in caring is to go slow. Men usually rush into first or second marriages sooner than women because they haven't learned to take care of themselves as women do. Mothers: Take the time to teach your sons to be self-reliant.

There are other options for the formerly married than to run out and get married again. In our society the church often looks upon the single as someone with deviant behavior. We usually are on the lookout to fix that single up with that perfect person.

The Bible makes it clear that singleness is a gift. In Matthew 19:3-8 Jesus relates that Moses permitted divorce because of the people's hardness of heart. The result of sin causes a disruption of God's original plan of marriage for life. The disciples in verse 10 suggest that it might be better not to marry, and Jesus in verse 11 points out that not everyone can do without marriage. Yet there are those who can, by nature and disposition, renounce marriage because it enables them to be more effective in the service of God.

The apostle Paul in 1 Corinthians 7:7,8 challenges the unmarried and widowed to consider the example he is setting. Paul declares the single state to be a gift.

He clearly states in 1 Corinthians 7:32-35 that the purpose of this gift is to enable the Christian to serve God without the distraction of marriage. Paul does warn that it is better to marry if you can't control your sexual passions.

In talking with many leaders of singles groups throughout America, their major concern is how to have their singles honor God's pattern of saving for marriage the most intimate of sexual relationships. They share how their people love the Lord, want to make God the Lord of their lives, are inspired by daily devotions, and trust in God's promises, but compromise their sexual drives as do people in the world.

It's important to remember that those who have been happily married for a long time often find that, though sexual relations are enjoyable, they can't begin to measure up to the intimacy that's found in the friendship and companionship of marriage. It takes time to nurture this kind of intimacy. Go slowly.

Since man is a social creature, he needs social contact. Friendship is one important form of social contact. Friendships are a viable alternative to those who have their passions under control. We all are aware that opposite-sex friendships can be difficult to maintain on a friendship level. A few points to keep in mind so that your contact remains on a strictly friendship factor are:

- See and treat this person as a brother or sister.

- Keep your focus on your mutual interests rather than upon each other.

- Keep your level of expectations at a low level.

- Welcome third and fourth parties in your relationship.

- Don't rely upon this person as your source of affirmation and emotional support.

- Keep your friendship at the appreciation level rather than at the affirmation or emotional level.

Filling the Void of Loneliness

When a relationship fails, it is so tempting to jump back into an involvement with another person because you feel so alone. This is not the time to fill the void, but rather to get a hold on your emotions. Two hurting people don't make a healthy relationship.

Carl Sandburg stated, "Shakespeare, Leonardo da Vinci, Benjamin Franklin, and Lincoln ... were not afraid of being lonely because they knew that was when the creative mood in them would work."[5] Use this phase of your life to begin a new career, write a book, give a speech, or sing a new song. There are several things you can do to fill this void of togetherness.

♥ *Keep busy:* Get in and solve those extra-hard jobs at home and work. Roll up your sleeves and get on it. Take that class you have always wanted to take at the local college: painting, sculpturing, cooking, design, computer, etc. Get involved in special-interest groups that you've never had time for. Your children are an excellent area of your life that needs extra time. This time of your life gives you a different perspective on what's important in life. Keeping busy means getting in touch with what you like to do.

♥ *Allow yourself time to grow:* Reevaluating your loss gives you an opportunity to find out who you are as a person. We must learn to be individuals again. Our culture doesn't always make it easy to function as a single. We are pressured into becoming a circle of two. Go slowly in developing new relationships. It's important to understand what went wrong so it won't be repeated. We need to know what we did to create problems in our previous relationships. Let's not carry this baggage into future partnerships.

♥ *Love yourself:* In Matthew 22:36-39 Jesus states the two most important commandments: to love the Lord your God with all your heart, soul, and mind and to love your neighbor as much as you love yourself. We live in a time where more is written and sung about love than during any other era in history, but we find ourselves not knowing how to love ourselves. We are to overcome loneliness by learning to like the company we keep: ourselves. Not only does the outward part of ourselves need to be loved, but also the inward part. Spend time getting to know yourself. There are probably several areas in your life that need paint and sprucing up.

One lady wrote and told me after attending one of my seminars that God had spoken to her about her excess weight, and that she was going to enter a nationally known weight-loss program to lose 100 pounds. One year later she came back with the report that she had lost 140 pounds and was feeling great about herself. Here was a woman who was beginning to love herself.

What action do you need to take to reflect your new love for yourself? Move out and do it.

♥ *Join a support group:* There are many outstanding groups formed to give you support during this time. Visit several groups before settling into any one. Make sure you find a group that meets your own needs and interests. Make sure it is positive in nature and that it will lift you up in your times together. Many times your own church will have a program to meet your needs. If not, ask your pastor for any recommendations. As a Christian I would highly recommend that you seek out a group that has spiritual (biblical Christianity) principles at work within its leadership. You will find God's principles of particular importance to you during this new season of your life.

♥ *Make new friends:* Through your support group, church, work, and leisure activities you will come into contact with a lot of new people, both male and female. Stay in multiple people encounters. Opposite-sex friendships are possible, but be honest with yourself and each other. Involve your children in these new friendships. They are also sensing a loss and need new role models and friends. Multiple friendships give you pleasurable contact with others without the commitments that intimacy demands. Go slowly with any new commitments. There is an excellent paperback regarding this topic. It is Alan Loy McGinnis' book entitled *The Friendship Factor*. He gives some very practical ideas on how to be a warmer, more lovable person, how to communicate better, and how to resolve tension in your relationships.

As we begin to realize that there are many people involved in this emerging group, we can become sensitive to their unique needs. What can the church do to show that it *cares*?

What the Church Can Do to Help

The eighties and nineties have been two decades of dramatic changes in the "Father Knows Best" stereotype of America's family. We are no longer a nation of the two-parent family with three children where the father is the breadwinner and the mother is the homemaker.

During these two decades we have been witnessing the single-parent explosion. Not only in our society in general but also within the church. Inner-city churches are particularly aware of this big swing. The suburban churches still sense the old family structure, but that profile is rapidly changing.

Our singles pastor, Roy Ronveaux, at Victoria Community Church has taken strong leadership in developing this new area of ministry. What was a small group a few years ago has grown manyfold because of our church's ministry in this area. Many of the other local churches will send their singles and singles with children to our church because we have a special program to minister to the uniqueness of this segment of our church population.

As a church we are to minister to all of our people. The singles ministry needs to differentiate between the single and the single parent. What can we do to maximize fitting singles into the complete body of the church?

- Become aware of the significant difference between singles and single parents.

- Be sensitive to the labels that are given to these groups.

- Include them in corporate worship and Bible study.

- Make allowances for differences for seminars, workshops, and socials.

- Make opportunities for involvement in mainstreaming and ministering to singles separately and as a group.

- Assess the needs of those in this group and design programs around these assessments.

- Provide programs that meet the needs of the unsaved and unchurched singles. The church has an excellent opportunity to reach this segment through their educational and child-care offerings.

- Create a newsletter to advertise the offerings of this group.

- Advertise in the local newspaper.

Andre Bustanoby in his book *Being a Single Parent* lists six mistakes to avoid if you want a successful singles ministry at your church:

1. *Lack of support and understanding by the senior pastor, church staff, and congregation at large.* Encouragement for the ministry must come from the top down. If the senior pastor doesn't take it [the singles ministry] seriously, why should anyone else? This doesn't mean that he must be involved actively or even directly promote it. He can use singles in general or single parents in particular in a positive way in his sermon illustrations. He can set aside a particular Sunday to recognize single parents. Does he view singles as whole people with lives and gifts of their own, or are they just in a holding pattern waiting to get married? Are single parents, particularly divorcées, an embarrassment, or are they capable of being adequate parents with the support of the church as an extended family?

2. *Lack of money because through lack of vision a singles ministry was not included in the budget.* An adequate singles program requires money. As pointed out earlier, a day-care center in the church facility is one way to fund a program for single parents.

Seminars, workshops, and groups that use marriage and family therapists and psychologists as leaders and facilitators can be operated on a pay-as-you-go basis. A modest registration fee could be charged to cover the speaker's expenses with a little money from the budget to cover any shortfall.

3. *Fad.* If a church is attempting to run a singles program because everyone has one, it is bound to fail. We don't start with a program; we start with a need and build a program to meet that need. The need may already exist in the church. It definitely exists in most communities, and your community can be reached by some imaginative, aggressive promotion.

4. *Lack of leadership.* Leaders are difficult to find. Good ones take responsibility and initiative with little prodding from the top. Leaders also require training. A leadership retreat is one way to develop leaders. Many men are discouraged from attending programs because too many women occupy leadership roles. Leadership needs to be divided between men and women.

5. *Lack of a balanced program.* A once-a-month potluck and a Sunday morning singles class is not a complete or balanced program. A balanced program includes Bible teaching, small-group discussions, a wide variety of social events, retreats, conferences, and specialty seminars. Give your leaders a chance to use new and innovative ideas.

6. *Lack of a long-range program.* Many groups have no idea what they are going to do more than two weeks in advance. If professionals or well-known speakers are going to participate effectively, they need to know in advance what is going to be done. A program that meets needs must have a plan of execution.[6]

As we begin to expand our vision of ministry to the body, may we become *carers* of the singles ministry. They make up a large segment of our church membership. Make them aware that God loves them and so do we. Give them assurance that they will fly again and soar high above the clouds.

John Donne so beautifully expresses the hope that we all have even in the midst of despair:

> He brought light out of darkness, not out of a lesser light; he can bring your summer out of winter, though you have no spring; though in the ways of fortune, or understanding, or conscience, you have been benighted until now, wintered and frozen, clouded and eclipsed, damped and benumbered, smothered and stupefied till now, now God comes to you, not as in the dawning of the day, not as in the bud of the spring, but as the sun at noon.[7]

———— ♥ ————

*Happiness is a
by-product of life.*

4 | *Caring About Children*

———————— ♥ ————————

*Behold, children are a gift of the Lord;
the fruit of the womb is a reward* (Psalm
127:3).

AS THIS CHAPTER BEGAN TO unfold in my mind, I was struck by a comment that Ravi Zakaris made one evening at Chuck Swindoll's church in Fullerton, California. As Ravi was sharing that evening he stated, "The most dangerous place for a young child today is in his mother's womb." As I thought about that statement, tears started to well up in my eyes and for the first time in my life I understood and agreed with that statement. You see, it was only a few years ago that I believed the opposite to be true in the American family. Yes, the womb used to be the safest place for a young child and now it's the most dangerous. How did that happen in just a few short years?

As I travel throughout America speaking, I talk to women who really try to focus on caring for their children. What a marvelous desire of the heart to love your children! As a young mother, God had impressed upon me a great desire to love and care for our children. It wasn't a curse to me but a blessing of trust that God would count me worthy to be trusted to care for one of His dear children.

"Being a parent is not something that people ever feel confident or secure about....We've always been a step behind in bringing you up."[1] So said Garrison Keillor, noted humorist and author, at a graduation ceremony for Gettysburg College in 1987.

Mr. Keillor sums it up well. Parenting is a tough job. It is something very few parents ever feel secure or confident about and, as advice and trends change, parents often fall a step behind.

Jesus, as He spent three years of ministry on this earth, spent a great deal of time caring for children. "But Jesus said, 'Let the children alone, and do not hinder them from coming to Me; for the kingdom of heaven belongs to such as these'" (Matthew 19:14). In many sections of the New Testament He is touching children, praising them, and admonishing adults to love and care for little children. He warned us not to harm them, because if we do the punishment will be severe.

One of the great women in American history was Sarah Edwards. Because of her love for her family, she had a great influence upon her family and also upon future generations.

———— ♥ ————

Sarah's vital interest in her children's development had a lasting impact. Married to the famous clergyman and theologian Jonathan Edwards, she was the mother of 11 children. At the same time, Sarah maintained a vital and intensely loving marriage.

Writing about the Edwards family, author Elizabeth Dodds says straightforwardly, "The way children turn out is always a reflection on their mother."

Dodds refers to a study done by A.E. Winship in 1900 in which he lists some of the accomplishments of the 1,400 Edwards descendants he located. The Edwards family produced:

13 college presidents
65 professors

100 lawyers and a dean of a law school
30 judges
66 physicians and a dean of a medical school
80 holders of public office
3 United States senators
3 mayors of large cities
3 state governors
1 vice president of the United States
1 controller of the United States Treasury

Winship believed that "much of the capacity and talent, intensity and character of the more than 1,400 of the Edwards family is due to Mrs. Edwards."

How did Sarah Edwards do it? A deeply Christian woman, Sarah emerges from the pages of Dodds' book as a firm, patient mother who treated her children with courtesy and love. Samuel Hopkins, a contemporary who spent time in the Edwards' household, said Sarah was able to guide her children without angry words or blows. Unlike many mothers today, Sarah had only to speak once and her children obeyed her.

"In their manners they were uncommonly respectful to their parents. When their parents came into the room, they all rose instinctively from their seats and never resumed them until their parents were seated."

These children who were so well-treated by their parents in turn loved and respected them as well as each other.

In the management of her busy colonial home, Sarah puts her modern counterparts to shame. We, who have only to press a button to start our many machines, can hardly imagine the sheer physical labor required of the colonial housewife. Sarah had many hard tasks: to see that the candles and clothes were made, the food prepared, the garden planted, the fire stoked, and the guests fed and comfortably housed. Contiguously, she taught her children to work and deal with life.

Dodds also portrays Sarah as a keen observer of human nature:

... [she] carefully observed the first appearance of resentment and ill will in her young children, toward any person whatever, and did not connive at... but was careful to show her displeasure and suppress it to the utmost; yet not by angry, wrathful words, which often provoke children to wrath.... Her system of discipline was begun at a very early age and it was her rule to resist the first, as well as every subsequent exhibition of temper or disobedience in the child... wisely reflecting that until a child will obey his parents, he will never be brought to obey God.

As a disciplinarian, Sarah clearly defined her boundaries and tolerated no misbehavior from her children. The result was a household that emanated love and harmony.

As Elizabeth Dodds makes abundantly clear in her book, a mother is not merely rearing her one generation of children. She is also affecting future generations for good or ill. All the love, nurture, education, and character-building that spring from Mother's work influence those sons and daughters. The results show up in the children's accomplishments, attitudes toward life and parenting capacity. For example, one of Sarah Edwards' grandsons, Timothy Dwight, president of Yale (echoing Lincoln) said, "All that I am and all that I shall be, I owe to my mother."

As one ponders this praise, the question arises: Are we women unhappy in our mothering role because we make too little, rather than too much, of that role? Do we see what we have to give our children as minor rather than major, and consequently send them into the world without a healthy core identity and strong spiritual values?

It was the great investment of time that mothers like Sarah Edwards and Susanna Wesley made in the lives of their children that garnered each such high praise. One can't teach a child to read in an hour or stretch a child's mind in a few days.

Have we as mothers unwisely left our children's education to school and church, believing that we can fill in
around the edges? And would we feel better about ourselves if we were more actively involved in teaching our
children? I think so.

A thread runs throughout the whole of life: Only as we
invest much will the yield be great. Our children are growing up in a rough, tough world, and they need us to invest a
lot of time and energy in their lives. Only then will they—
and we—experience significant gain.[2]

If only there were more women like Sarah Edwards! We
would not have to spend hours upon hours undoing the
wrongs of our society. We wouldn't have to spend billions of
dollars each year trying to mend lives that have been
destroyed because of women's and men's hardness of
heart. How did Sarah find the time, energy, and money to
be involved with her family? She voluntarily chose to!
There are only 24 hours in a day for all of us. We do what we
want to do. In Psalm 90:17 the writer challenges us to know
the "work of our hands." That verse has really challenged
me to delve into God's Word to see what is really the work
of a woman's hands.

I have come to the conclusion that Satan has prevented
the American woman from seeing what God originally
planned for women at creation. As the famous song of
yesteryear so aptly asks, "Where have all the flowers
gone?" We might ask, "Where have all the mothers gone?"
When we find godly women, we should sing their praises
from the housetops. They should be raised up to teach and
share their God-given wisdom. Instead, our society makes
them feel like second-rate citizens because they aren't
more ambitious than to stay home with such a boring task.
We aren't proud to be homemakers anymore. To be worthy

we think we must have a career and work outside our homes.

However, as the decade of the nineties begins, I can see some changes in this stereotype of the American woman. I hear from women who are beginning to say, "It's not worth it anymore. I am not going to be depressed because I can't do it all. I want more of what God had in mind when He originally made me." How did our families get overextended? As a young bride and mother I certainly sensed a slower pace for all of us. We had more time for the important things of life. What caused the change?

An Overview

As we review the past, we can begin to identify the major differences between then and the present.

For hundreds of years, children were raised in the traditions and lifestyles of their parents. As we adjusted to those elements within our lifestyle, we reflected a relative stability within our families.

If our families were farmers, we became farmers. If they were bakers, we became bakers. If they were tailors, we also became tailors. There was very little departure from this. As children we used our childhood to learn the skills and trade of our parents. The boys patterned themselves after their fathers and the girls imitated the homemaking skills of Mom.

With the advent of the "baby boomers" just after World War II, many families moved away from grandmothers, grandfathers, aunts, uncles, cousins, nieces, and nephews. They moved from small, rural towns to large, urban and suburban cities. Not only did we move, but we kept moving, again, again, and again. Today, our families move almost every $2^{1}/_{2}$ years.

Very rare is the family who has lived in the same area for 20-30 years. In many cases we are lucky to know our neighbors before it is time to move.

In times before 1946, children were able to learn their life skills through on-the-job training because they were needed to help the family function properly and survive. In the larger cities children weren't able to help the family function properly. Dad went to work, usually far from home, and the children weren't even aware what Dad did, let alone where he worked. As our society was becoming more consumer-oriented, dads worked longer hours and in many cases took on a second job so the family could get that bigger home, second car, a nicer summer vacation, the new-style television, and even a dishwasher. Once we tasted materialism, Mom even got the idea things could come faster and in bigger packages if she could go to work like Dad.

As the children came home to the empty house, they began to spend more and more time in front of the television set. Many times the programs were counterproductive to what parents believed and were teaching their children.

In 1990 larger numbers of children have fewer and fewer opportunities to have a meaningful role in family life and traditions. *Without a meaningful role, it is difficult to develop a sense of meaning, purpose, and significance through being needed, listened to, and taken seriously.*

If our family is to survive in the form we so highly value, we must recapture the strengths of our previous historical families. Somehow we must find time and opportunities to train our children to have skills that make them have a meaningful attitude toward being a member of our family. When our granddaughter Christine (aged 6) comes over to Grammy Em's home, I review with her what she can do. I say to her, "Christine, tell me all you can do." She lists things like bathe myself, dress myself, make my bed, walk to school by myself, help Mommy fold the clothes, feed Dori (their dog), dust the furniture, make a salad, scramble eggs, set the table, load the dishwasher, etc. I go through this little game all the time because I want her to realize she can do a lot of things around her home and that she has significance and worth to our family. I do the same with Chad and Bevan, but to a lesser degree because they are younger. I also want them to realize that they are needed. Each family differs, however. I challenge you as moms to plan ways in which your children can verbalize what they can do. We all need to be needed. Oh yes, many times we as moms can do it better and faster, but they will never learn to be significant and needed if we do everything for them.

Being listened to is also an area that we must plan if we are to teach the valuable skill of communication. I have found that if we don't take time to listen to our children, they will find other people who will. In most cases these people will not reflect our same values. If we listen to our children, they will be more apt to listen to us.

A lady in Sacramento told me recently that every evening while the children are preparing for bed she talks with the children about their day. They have a little game each evening which goes like this, "What was the best thing that happened to you today?" Each person recites what was the best thing for him or her. She says she is amazed at what is shared. Other couples use this same technique around the dinner table. In this way, Dad gets to participate in telling what was best for him, too. Dads make a big difference in developing values for the children.

In Deuteronomy 6:7 it states, "And [you] shall talk of them when you sit in your house and when you walk by the way and when you lie down and when you rise up." Use every opportunity to teach your children. As the children get older they must know that their thoughts are taken seriously. Do they have a say in helping select weekend outings and where to go for that summer vacation? What about giving them a voice in the color and make of the family automobile and in choosing the neighborhood in which the family will live? Children will make meaningful contributions if as parents we care.

"In times of change, learners inherit the earth, while the learned find themselves beautifully equipped to deal with a world that no longer exists,"[3] states Eric Hoffer.

We are certainly in a world of change with a greater speed of change than any time in history. In order for us to adapt, we must be learners. If we stop reading, thinking, and attending growth seminars, we will be like the dinosaurs of old—extinct. My Bob gives this quote in our Working Woman's Seminar: "What you will be in the next five years will depend upon two things. One, the people you meet, and two, the books you read." Surround yourself with good people and good books. As John Wesley so aptly stated, "Reading Christians are growing Christians. When Christians cease to read, they cease to grow."[4]

Walt Disney said there were three types of people: the well poisoners, the lawn mowers, the life enhancers.

The *well poisoners* are always negative—everything is bad and tomorrow we will be destroyed. They think the worst and proclaim that life isn't worth living. The *lawn mowers* are satisfied with the status quo. "It was good enough for Grandpa, so it is good enough for me. We've done it this way for 20 years—why change now?" This type of person doesn't recognize change, denies that it exists, and won't recognize its presence. Stay away from them—they have no new and stimulating thoughts. The *life enhancers* are the people who are alive and well. Grab on to them; they will take you to the action. They try to give life away. The more they give, the more they get. These people will take you to new heights of challenge and change. You won't become a dinosaur; instead you will find yourself continually being reborn as a butterfly.

My heart's desire is that we will all become life enhancers. Sarah Edwards produced new life by giving hers away. When we begin to care for our children, we will begin to see that life is worth living. Will there be any setbacks, disappointments, and failures? Yes—on a regular basis. But it's worth it.

Families in Transition

Up through World War II, life was very hard for most American families. Each member of the family had to work hard to scratch out a daily living. Each person was desirous of making a better life. Education was a prized commodity. We knew that if we were to escape our present condition we had to get a good education. It was a privilege to go to school. It surely beat the hard work on the farm. Yet hard times developed character qualities in our children that were positive in nature: self-discipline, perseverance, responsibility, willingness to be hard-working, honor, good judgment, and trustworthiness.

Things drastically changed after World War II. We became a country of people seeking self-indulgence. As we became affluent and more oriented to things, our children no longer felt the need to contribute and be self-reliant. School became boring and irrelevant. Children wanted immediate gratification in life and turned to alcohol, drugs, sex, and more and more time in front of the television and high-tech gadgets. They became disrespectful, depressed, sullen, and suicidal in behavior. The high school achievement scores reflected this changed attitude and began to sink lower and lower at an alarming rate. Over the years our youth have lost the values that our early forefathers had when they came to this country. Many of these early discoverers would risk their lives to get aboard a crowded boat and come to America. On the West Coast we are seeing in various Oriental immigrants the same values for hard work, family unity, and commitment that our early forefathers exhibited.

In many cases in our local high schools we find that our traditional students are ill-prepared to be competitive on the high school and college campuses. Our challenge today is to help our children develop the self-reliance, commitment, and skills that children learned as a matter of course 30 to 50 years ago. In those days childhood was an internship for life.

In contrast to the old days, our children at the onset of puberty face a great many challenges but have a deficiency in capabilities. Today's children will be forced to accept more years of education than most people in history could ever dream of having. And to many of our young people, education will seem like a curse. With the passing of values we once held dear and with the urban revolution, we witnessed some drastic changes in our family structure. Families moved from living rooms filled with dialogue to family rooms controlled by electronic devices. As a result conversation became limited. Once we had kitchens filled with rituals, tradition, and colorations, and supper table conversations extending until bedtime. Now we have rooms full of machines that pour noise and images into our homes and wipe out all personal interaction. Recently I received a letter from Melinda in Florida. She writes:

Dear Emilie,

Thank you so very much for your book *Survival for Busy Women*. I have read it twice and find myself really challenged by the writing and I find that I really want to make major changes in my life. I have a couple of questions regarding your chapter on goal setting (pages 20-21). You state under long-range goals for family that you want to have teenage children who can carry on an interesting conversation with adults and to have children who sit in with adults and discuss contemporary topics relating to current events. I, too, want those goals but how do I teach them to my children?

As soon as my children and husband come home they turn on the TV very loud and escape into those programs for the rest of the evening. There is no conversation unless an argument arises about what program is next. They don't even want to come to the dinner table for meals. They take plates in front of the TV and lap-eat.

I'm so discouraged I can't keep my composure at times. I need help. I want to be a good mother and wife, but I get no help around the home. Any suggestions will be appreciated.

Keep up your good works unto the Lord.

—Melinda
St. Petersburg, Florida

There are many families in this same situation all over America. The electronic media have invaded our homes and we are the losers. As parents we must come together as a team and preserve conversation in our homes. These few hours each day are our only time to transmit the values of our generation to the next.

While our children are young, we need to teach them selective viewing that would limit the time and topic of TV programs watched. Consider allowing no TV until homework is completed and no TV during meals, and insisting on the family sharing meals together whenever possible (soft dinner music in the home can be relaxing and soothing to jangled nerves). As parents we must have a plan or we won't meet long-range goals.

In 1940 at least one grandparent was a full-time active member of approximately 60-70% of all households. Today fewer than 2% of our families have a grandparent available as a helper. In the same year a full-time homemaker spent approximately thirty-nine hours a week on domestic engineering chores in more than 90% of all households. Today close to 88% of all children who return home from school enter a household where every living member has been gone for the best ten hours of the day. Once the family assembles, all the routine business of the household is still to be done. It takes an average of thirty-seven hours a week to accomplish the domestic chores but in most households there is no one around all day to do them.

The need to get chores done after a long day at work competes with any remaining time for high-quality interaction. By the time we scurry around putting food on the table, washing and sorting clothes, taking care of other chores, issuing warnings, perhaps spending a moment in the tub, the day is over. If we are not careful, we sacrifice two things we can not afford to lose—the dialogue and collaboration that affirms our sense of ourselves.[5]

In this transition we left behind rituals, traditions, culture, social networks, and support systems and we became isolated from one another. When Bob and I first founded "More Hours in My Day," our motivation wasn't from the findings of research. God motivated us by giving us a hunger to teach fast-disappearing values in our seminars. In each of five seminars we give basic and creative ways in which parents can make an impact upon their families by teaching those things that have been lost in making the big changes from yesteryear to the future. They are:

- Providing dialogue in our homes.

- Collaboration of each family member's value to the family.

- Creating and continuing to develop rituals and traditions.

- Providing a network for teaching cultural and social values.

- Developing support systems that prevent us from being isolated.

And we thought being a parent was going to be easy! As Eric Hoffer stated, "We had to continue to be learners."[6] Over the years the growth of our ministry has been the result of God's blessing on our materials and also the affirmation that what is being taught meets the needs of mothers and women who are searching for basic answers to "How do I do it?"

What Builds Strength in a Family

As Bob and I have enjoyed 35 years of marriage, raised two children, and talked to thousands of women, we have observed certain characteristics that seem to account for the success, happiness, and strength of families in America:

1. An awareness that each member of the family feels appreciated.

2. A voluntary desire to spend quantity and quality time together.

3. Good communication patterns among family members.

4. A high degree of religious orientation within the family.

5. A strong commitment to make the family unit succeed.

6. The ability to deal with crisis situations in a positive manner.

As we have continually read available research data regarding the family, we find that these characteristics are often stated as vital components of successful families. Our observations would support these characteristics, too.

In our "Growing a Great Marriage" seminars we express these observations to the audiences, trying to shorten the couples' lead time in figuring out what the program is all about. I trust the following comments, observations, and techniques will help you as a reader sift through what's important and begin an active program of incorporating these characteristics into your family structure.

Appreciation

The letter "A" is such an edifying letter of the alphabet, beginning words like "acceptance," "adoration," and "appreciation." If by the power of God we could wake up each morning to the idea that we were going to be a blessing to members of our family, and no matter what we were going to practice the "three A's", we would have such an impact that we would turn our families and the world upside down. Each of us cries out, "Does anyone appreciate me?" Moms seek kind words regarding meals, laundry, mending, nursing, mothering, and wifing. Wouldn't moms love to hear and know they are appreciated? Rather than trying to flee the role of wife and mother, Mom would get such great satisfaction from God's plan that she would stand in the kitchen and be called "blessed."

What about Dad's need of knowing the family appreciates all that he does by consistently going to his place of business, sacrificing to come home on time, fighting the freeway stress, and participating at church and school when needed? If dads were told that they were doing a good job, they would be so excited they couldn't wait to get home to the family. No working overtime to escape, or on weekends to get away from the family. No dropping by the bars, but a real excitement to be where the real action is—*home.*

Our youth counselors tragically point out in painful statistics what happens to our children when they don't feel accepted—low grades, runaways, sex, alcohol, drugs, abortion, and loss of personal worth. Our children cry out in various ways, asking painfully, "Does anyone appreciate me? Do I make a difference in my family or will it even exist after I'm gone?" What changed lives we'd see if our children only knew we cared and that they play a vital part in who our family is! Often we think it's only important while they are young, but as a mother of a son who will be 30 and a daughter who will be 32, that need goes on and on.

One evening we were at our daughter's home for dinner and we were having appetizers and talking around the snack bar when Bob asked our granddaughter, Christine, to come and sit on his lap. Jenny spoke up and asked her father, "Why don't you ask me to sit on your lap anymore?" Bob was taken back for a moment because he thought she was too old to sit in her dad's lap anymore. But with great sensitivity, Bob put his arms around her waist and cuddled her into his lap. Our children always need to be appreciated and loved, no matter how old they become.

Write a card or letter to a member of your family today and share how much you appreciate what they mean to you and the family. It will only cost a little time and a few cents, but it will reap marvelous dividends for years to come. To this day we share words of encouragement with all members of our family through direct words, on the telephone, or in a letter. We stress the three A's continually. Dare to ask a very searching question: "Do you know you are appreciated?"

Spending Time Together

We humbly stated as our children were growing up that there was not going to be a generation gap in our family. We decided that we were going to make our family an exciting place to be around—more fun than any peer group activities. Oh, sure, there were many activities at church and school that we weren't invited to, but we were there in spirit rooting them on. In my various books I have shared with my readers how Bob and I dedicated ourselves to their activities from elementary school through college.

One activity that paid great "togetherness dividends" was our Family Conference Time. See pages 195-201 in my *Survival for Busy Women* book (Harvest House Publishers). I go into great detail describing how this time worked in our family. We always knew that, no matter what, our home was a "trauma center" and you didn't have to be perfect to be a member. For many years a segment of our society expressed a little saying, "I'm okay and you're okay," but we went one step further and said, "I'm not okay, but that's okay." As sinners we wanted our family to recognize the grace of God and His forgiveness. It's okay not to be perfect. Families have lost the sense of a balanced life and how to live in moderation. We have become such an addictive and compulsive society. This last Christmas our son gave his Dad a white T-shirt with the word *MODERATION* silk-screened on the front. Brad said when he saw that shirt he just had to get it for Dad. In our many times together over the years, Dad kept sharing "moderation, moderation" until it became part of Brad's lifestyle. Many family experts emphasize that the best place to experience this healthy characteristic of spending time together is outdoor camping. This activity seems to have all of the components that bond families together. It includes goal selection, pre-planning, budgeting, working together as a team, food preparation, stress involved in solving problems, cleanup, and adjusting to the unexpected and unusual. Yes, camping has it all. If a family can spend a few days or a few weeks together in the outdoors, they can certainly adjust to the everyday living conditions at home with all the modern conveniences. As we spend time together, we will begin to develop those memories that will last us for the rest of our lives. Laughter in a family is healthy to the soul. Bob and I vividly remember the quietness of our home when we were alone after such events as a birthday party with all the children and their friends, a large gathering for Thanksgiving and Christmas, and even a wedding reception. Yet if we were very still, we could still hear the echoes of laughter in the walls.

Maintaining a sense of humor between Mom, Dad, and the children can be a great adventure. Bob Benson in his book *Laughter in the Walls* captures the essence of spending time together in laughter as a family.

LAUGHTER IN THE WALLS

I pass a lot of houses on my way home—
some pretty,
    some expensive,
      some inviting—
but my heart always skips a beat
   when I turn down the road
and see my house nestled against the hill.
   I guess I'm especially proud
of the house and the way it looks because
   I drew the plans myself.
It started out large enough for us—
   I even had a study—
two teenaged boys now reside in there.
   And it had a guest room—
my girl and nine dolls are permanent guests.
   It had a small room Peg
had hoped would be her sewing room—
   the two boys swinging on the dutch door
have claimed this room as their own.
   So it really doesn't look right now
as if I'm much of an architect.
   But it will get larger again—
one by one they will go away
   to work,
      to college,
   to service,
   to their own houses,
and then there will be room—
   a guest room,
     a study,
   and sewing room
   for just the two of us.
But it won't be empty—
   every corner
     every room

every nick
   in the coffee table
will be crowded with memories.
Memories of picnics,
   parties, Christmases,
   bedside vigils, summers,
     fires, winters, going barefoot,
leaving for vacation, cats,
   conversations, black eyes,
graduations, first dates,
   ball games, arguments,
washing dishes, bicycles,
   dogs, boat rides,
getting home from vacation,
   meals, rabbits and
a thousand other things
   that fill the lives
of those who would raise five.
And Peg and I will sit
quietly by the fire
and listen to the
laughter in the walls.[7]

When the children are gone, no lunches are to be made, and retirement sets in—what will you hear in your walls? I pray it's laughter, for God created laughter as well as tears for our lives.

Good Communication Patterns

Around our home we have a trademark expression, "Is that edifying?" taken from Ephesians 4:29:

Let no unwholesome word proceed from your mouth, but only such a word as is good for edification according to the need of the moment, that it may give grace to those who hear.

We are very conscious that our words are to be:

- Wholesome
- Edifying
- Providing grace to the hearer

Florence Littauer, our very close personal friend, has written a new book entitled *Silver Boxes with Bows*, which gives many illustrations of how people have used this verse of Scripture to be an encouragement to others. She shares so clearly that our words can be positive and negative, and the Scriptures certainly encourage us to be positive in our speech.

Even as young children, Brad and Jenny knew that we were a family of encouragers. We not only stressed proper talking techniques, but we also stressed what it took to be a good listener: Someone who listened not only with ears but also with the heart.

Our children participated in adult conversation from the very beginning. We wanted them to feel comfortable around our adult friends. They were welcomed to offer comments when appropriate. Many times they would just listen, but as they got older they began to enter in with feelings and opinions. What great wisdom comes out of the mouths of babes! They would astonish us with their depth of questioning and reasoning.

This was the time we taught manners, thoughtfulness, and courtesies. No question was too dumb or thoughtless. We had many laughs *with* each other, but not *at* another member of the family.

One thing we have lost from our culture of the past is the custom of eating a meal around the family table. An important word needs to reappear in our families: *dialogue*.

In 1970, the average American watched television for five hours per day. When we add those five hours to work time, commuting time, and sleep, it leaves only one hour for potential family interaction. This doesn't count mealtimes and the normal business of the family. So we got very creative. We combined our mealtime and TV viewing time at the expense of all the sharing that in pre-television times was the norm at the dinner table. So when do we talk? If we use 45 minutes of the remaining hour every day for routine duties, 15 minutes are left over for meaningful dialogue. In 20 years we have gone from a society with a surplus of significant communication among the generations to a society in which that kind of significant interaction is the rare exception.

Research is now confirming that dialogue and collaboration form the foundations of moral and ethical development, critical thinking, judgmental maturity, and teaching effectiveness. Conversely, lack of dialogue and collaboration between the more mature and less mature threatens the bonds of closeness, trust, dignity, and respect that hold our society together.

As a result of the scarcity of dialogue and collaboration in our homes and schools, a serious crisis has arisen in our culture. When adults lecture, instruct, explain, or moralize as their primary teaching methods, young people turn away, running instead to their peer groups as their primary source in their learning and identity-forming activities.

When peers dialogue with peers, all they achieve is naive clarity. Peers means "those at the same level of insight, awareness, and maturity." By definition, young people are incapable of informing themselves of all they need to know to become mature adults. How could they possibly alert themselves to the need for learning that of which they are completely unaware? It is only when more mature people—siblings, parents, relatives, teachers, neighbors, and other community members—collaborate with young people in learning situations, and then through dialogue encourage them to develop and clarify their thinking, that young people mature and gain a sense of discernment and judgment.[8]

If we are to have an impact on our children we must, underline *must*, spend valuable time with them. The research evidence states that if we don't dialogue with our children we will lose them to other forces in our society. We must dialogue with our children if we are going to have an impact upon their lives. Proverbs 22:6 commands, "Train up a child in the way he should go, even when he is old he will not depart from it." We have to have proper communication patterns at work in our families.

Religious Orientation Within the Family

The church plays a large part in developing a support group for individuals in the family. It not only gives spiritual instruction, but also provides clean and healthy activities for children. As our society becomes more complex, we find our churches beginning to offer activities that weren't offered in the past. Not only is the church ministering to its members' needs, but it also offers assistance to those outside the church.

As Bob and I look back over the training years of our children, we say time and time again we could not have done it without help from the church. It was the source for teaching us how to be godly parents. Proverbs 24:3,4 was a pillar for our guidance: "By wisdom a house is built, and by understanding it is established; and by knowledge the rooms are filled with all precious and pleasant riches." This verse stressed to us that we needed three aspects of awareness to raise our children: *wisdom*, *understanding*, and *knowledge*. The church was the basic source from which to gain the necessary ingredients for putting our family together.

Mary from Pasadena, California, wrote me a letter recently confirming how our seminars have challenged her to reawaken her dormant faith. She thanked me for renewing her interest in spirituality. She stated that her teenage son and daughter have gotten involved with the high school department and her husband has gone to several men's activities and really likes them. She writes, "Our family has never been so together. Thanks, Emilie, for your encouragement."

If you aren't presently involved as a person or family in religious activities, I really challenge you in this area. Your participation will become a very valuable part of having a strong family. If you aren't familiar with any local churches, I might suggest that you ask friends, neighbors, or people at work for their recommendations. Then take a few weeks to visit the various churches in your area and see which one you are most compatible with.

Commitment

This word has lost its original meaning in our present society. In the old days, it meant just that—no matter what, we are bonded together. Our marriage vows contain lines of commitment "for richer, for poorer, in sickness and in health, until death do us part." These words used to mean something; today we are not so sure. Even leaders in sports, church, and politics don't mean what they say or what they signed in a contract. It's all relative.

The family which endures through good times and bad times is the one whose members are committed to each other. Two key words are "with" and "for." The various members of our families need to know that we are "with them" and "for them"—no matter what. They need to hear, "I'm with you unconditionally!" When wives and children see that Dad is committed to his marriage and family, it is such a freeing experience for the family. The members of the family don't have to waste energy or thought wondering where Dad is in the family relationship. They know he is *committed*. The same holds true for Mom. The greatest bond for a successful family is to have two loving parents who are committed to marriage, family, and home.

Dealing with Crisis Situations in a Positive Manner

Our last observation in what characterizes a strong family is the ability to handle crisis situations in a positive manner. The family that is transparent enough to let all sorts of events happen in their lives and yet maintain a strong, positive attitude is very desirous. One key verse of Scripture is found in Romans 8:28: "And we know that God causes all things to work together for good to those who love God, to those who are called according to His purpose." We know from experience that all things have worked for our good in life. In many events during our lives we have thought that God was closing the door on certain events, not realizing that He was opening a new window in this event called "life."

We must begin to see that all events fall into God's master plan. He has given us a higher calling than the world knows anything about. Each event is a piece of the jigsaw puzzle that helps to unlock the meaning of life.

If family members show appreciation, like to spend time together, exhibit good communication patterns, are committed to the family, have a high degree of religious orientation, and have the ability to deal with crises in a positive manner, I can guarantee that this family will be successful.

We as parents must use wisdom, understanding, and knowledge to develop a plan to care for our children and family. If we do, they will stand and call us blessed.

Recently I came across a very interesting book that contained an essay about the simpleness of life. The essay expresses what the really important things in life are all about. If we could only master these elements, we would truly have succeeded in figuring out what makes for success in caring for our children and family:

——————— ♥ ———————

ALL I EVER REALLY NEEDED TO KNOW I LEARNED IN KINDERGARTEN

Most of what I really need to know about how to live, and what to do, and how to be, I learned in kindergarten. Wisdom was not at the top of the graduate school mountain but there in the sandbox at nursery school.

These are the things I learned: Share everything. Play fair. Don't hit people. Put things back where you found them. Clean up your own mess. Don't take things that aren't yours. Say you're sorry when you hurt someone. Wash your hands before you eat. Flush. Warm cookies and cold milk are good for you. Live a balanced life. Learn some and think some and draw and paint and sing and dance and play and work some every day.

Take a nap every afternoon. When you go out into the world, watch for traffic, hold hands, and stick together. Be aware of wonder. Remember the little seed in the plastic cup. The roots go down and the plant goes up and nobody really knows how or why, but we are all like that.

Goldfish and hamsters and white mice and even the little seed in the plastic cup—they all die. So do we.

And then, remember the book about Dick and Jane and the first word you learned, the biggest word of all: LOOK. Everything you need to know is in there somewhere. The Golden Rule and love and basic sanitation. Ecology and politics and sane living.

Think of what a better world it would be if we all—the whole world—had cookies and milk about 3 o'clock every afternoon and then lay down with our blankets for a nap. Or if we had a basic policy in our nation and other nations to always put things back where we found them and cleaned up our own messes. And it is still true, no matter how old you are, when you go out into the world it is best to hold hands and stick together.[9]

——————— ♥ ———————

One woman's father began to realize these basic truths and wrote a belated letter with a gift to his beloved daughter and shared a magic moment from the past. She had to share this precious event with me.

Dear Emilie,

Before I share with you a letter I received from my dad, I wanted to give a little background so you would realize just how much it meant to me. A few years ago my parents divorced after nearly 30 years of marriage. (I am the oldest of four children.) Needless to say, so many things changed, particularly my role as a daughter. My life seemed turned upside down. The relationship between my dad and I was strained for a while. Although I never stopped loving him, our relationship would never be the same again. I have done a lot of growing and learning over the years since.

Just before Christmas, I received an unexpected package in the mail. Enclosed in the package was a letter with the following instructions: "Sheri, you wanted one of these a long time ago! Explanation enclosed, read *before* opening." Here is the letter.

——————— ♥ ———————

Dear Sheri,

You didn't know it but last night you and I shared a *magic* moment together. . . . I stopped at a very small "shoppe" in town to browse. It was pretty cold and breezy, and the owner had a fire going in her pot-bellied stove in the corner. The room wasn't too well lit and everything was old (well if not old, at least used) and it smelled a little musty... the kind of place you might envision in a movie.

After finding nothing of real interest, I spotted the enclosed item on my way out. I was immediately transported back in time to a similar evening when just you and I went "looking"... (I couldn't afford to buy anything then)... and I *remembered* that wonderful way you had of seeing all the beautiful parts of the world with big, bright eyes and smiles (you were maybe five or six months old). That made me feel as if we were both in a fairy tale... (one nice thing about being older is that you can let a tear fall in public and people seem to understand)! Well, in short, this obviously *belongs to you*.... Sorry it took so long! I guess you will always be my bright-eyed baby.

Love, Daddy

———— ♥ ————

Although my dad wasn't aware of all I had been going through with the changes in our family, and the confusion I felt, I'm sure he somehow sensed my need for this declaration of love. I will cherish the letter always. (By the way, the gift was a musical "Dickens" box, the kind you shake up and it snows.)

—Sheri Torelli
Riverside, California

———— ♥ ————

People find joy
by investing themselves
in others.

5 | Things Happen When Women Care to Clean

---♥---

Everything I didn't do yesterday
added to everything I haven't done today
Plus everything I won't do tomorrow
completely exhausts me!

*T*HE MINISTRY OF "More Hours In My Day" was the beginning direction God gave me over 12 years ago. From that came my first book by the same title (Harvest House Publishers). My expertise in organization was truly a God-given talent. I never set out to teach women and lead seminars. By teaching my own experiences, I found that women were encouraged and surprisingly helped. I realized that if women could incorporate simple ideas and methods they could have more hours for family and themselves, and get more out of life by having time to serve the Lord. Here is a letter I received:

Dear Emilie,

It has been a real joy and pleasure to read *Survival for Busy Women.* I am a mother of two boys, ages 2 and 5. I have been both a Business Education teacher and a secretary in the past. In addition to needing organization skills to survive running a household and raising our children (as all mothers do), it is very much a part of my personality to strive to be organized and efficient. My mother was not at all organized and efficient. I have always had the potential to be like her but have always done what I could to prevent that from happening. I am very organized in many areas. I also have areas that really need to be "cleaned up." So, your Total Mess to Total Rest plan, along with many other suggestions from your book will be put to good use in this particular household. During July and August I spent a lot of time reading your book, setting goals from "10-year goals" right down to "today's goals" in many areas (spiritual, marital, children, church, personal, physical, etc.) and thinking and planning ways that I can get "caught up" so that I can "keep up."

Thank you, Mrs. Barnes, for all the tips! You are my kind of woman! Praise God for all that He has done in your life and how He is using you in the lives of others. I want to make the best use of my time so that I am available for the Lord to be used in His kingdom in whatever way He wants to use me—*I want to become the woman that God wants me to be!* Thanks for the encouragement!

—Karen
Andover, New Jersey

Time management is personal. Each individual and every family situation is different. But the guidelines for getting the most out of your time are universal. We all have 24 hours in a day and 365 days in a year. Personal goals and schedules vary, but our days are numbered the same.

When we analyze our use of time, especially our home-making hours, we can determine our goals, develop our own time plan, use step savers, and try new ways. Be committed to act now and do it.

Let's think about those things, *plan them*, and *work them*. You'll soon discover you have more time to do the things you really want to do—more time to spend on projects, career, family, and spiritual growth (not necessarily in that order).

Dear Emilie,

I have just completed reading your books *The Creative Home Organizer*, *Survival for Busy Women*, and *More Hours in My Day*. These books are very encouraging and I want to thank you for sharing the great organizational skills God has blessed you with.

I am a Christian wife, mother, and executive secretary every day of the year. It seems as though there is never enough of me to go around. While my home is the most precious part of my life, it seems to suffer the most.

My husband is a three-year-old Christian and is still learning God's intended role for him in our home. Although I love being at home, he has encouraged me to work. I have been blessed to stay at home awhile when my daughter was small. I only have one child and she has just started her freshman year at high school. Since we have no savings at all for her college, my husband and I both feel I must work to put money back, for this expense is right around the corner.

But our home is so chaotic, clutter everywhere, late suppers, stacked laundry (clean and dirty). Not to mention the biggies like dirty carpet, blinds, closets, garage. I did not have a happy home growing up and I feel like I am cheating myself and my daughter out of much precious time right now in order to provide for her needs later down the road. As I mentioned, there was a time I stayed at home and our life was so much richer. The house was so peaceful, clean, and cozy. My attitude was much calmer and more lighthearted. The only problem I had was we could not pay the bills.

Please pray for me to grow in faith and organization.

—Sandy
Spring, Texas

When I received this letter from Sandy, I felt her frustration. Hopefully, Sandy, this chapter—along with my other books—will help you see the light at the end of the tunnel. I know God will honor your heart.

One of the most frequent questions asked at our seminars is "What kind of list is available for areas to be cleaned and maintained for each room of my home?" Now some of you are saying, "What a silly question! Everyone knows what to clean and how to do it." Wrong. The young women of the past two decades are the major women attending More Hours in My Day seminars. They hardly have a clue as to what to do, where to begin, and how to do it. These women went to college, built a career, married, and now have husbands, homes, and children. Many were not taught at home or given an example to follow. I've found this to be true across the United States and Canada.

Did you ever think how important it is to make every move count when housecleaning? That means to work around the room once and not backtrack. Start at the sink going from left to right or right to left, whichever feels good to you, and work from top to bottom—always. No exceptions. Vertical surfaces are never as dirty as horizontal surfaces. Think about it—upper shelves have less dirt than lower shelves. Check it out—the ceiling is cleaner than the floor. The number-one rule is to get organized with the proper tools. I use a plastic carryall tray. This is my permanent storage for all my equipment. It holds cleanser, window spray, heavy-duty spray, furniture polish, feather duster, scraper or razor blades, dust cloths (100 percent cotton—diapers are perfect), whisk broom, toothbrush, pumice stone, and rubber gloves. These items go with me from room to room. The secret is to work fast and smart. Put on some fast, upbeat music. This helps you to speed up and takes your mind off the drudgery.

Next comes your list of what needs cleaning and when. Don't clean something if it isn't dirty. The lists at the end of this chapter will help you determine which items to clean and how often they need cleaning. The lists are pretty complete and can be posted for the family to check items off as they're completed. Adapt the checklist to your own home and lifestyle.

Solicit your family's help and work as a team. Have everyone over 8 years old clean and straighten his own room. Teach them your method of top to bottom and left to right. They can also help vacuum, dust, polish, etc. This will save the harder jobs for the older members of the family. You may want to organize and straighten storage and linen closets. Our 5-year-old grandson, Chad, loves to organize the placemat shelf. His little hands are capable, and he does a very good job. Remember to praise, praise, praise. It will get you happy attitudes for future jobs.

For the single person, household chores may need to be done only by you. Or you may want to trade and share with another single. It's always more fun to work with someone.

Keep track of your time and how long each job or room takes. As you practice from week to week, you'll get faster.

If your time is limited, which it seems to be for most people, do cleaning in time slots—20 minutes in the morning and 20 minutes in the evening until the chores are done. *It's better to do something than nothing. A little headway every day will get you a long way.*

Use both hands. This may take some practice, but you'll get done faster. Spray with one hand and dust with the other hand. Finish one step with one hand and start the next step with the other. Why should one hand do all the work? God gave us the perfect equipment, so let's use our hands to work together and not be idle with one.

I love my feather duster. Used properly it can be a real time-saver for you. Invest in a good ostrich duster. Hardware stores or janitorial supply stores carry them. Real ostrich feathers work the best.

The dust in a house does need to be controlled as much as possible. Your feather duster is used to maintain a basically clean house on a regular basis. If you use slow motions and try not to flip your duster from side to side, the dust will adhere to the feathers and what doesn't will fall to the floor where you'll be vacuuming it up—remember, we're cleaning top to bottom. If you have heavy dust, you may need to vacuum the surface first and/or wipe the dust up with a cloth and polish.

Many of my ideas have come from my own trial-and-error experiences. Many have also come from a super book by Jeff Campbell, *Speed Cleaning*, which I highly recommend. It can be purchased from our order form. See page 252 for details.

Your feather duster is the perfect tool for those mini-blinds. Here is the method I use (it's also recommended in Jeff Campbell's book). Lower your blinds full length. Turn slats to the closed position. Grasp the cord that runs through them and pull the blinds away from the window. Reach behind them with your feather duster using long, downward strokes, top to bottom. Go slowly, stopping your duster at the bottom in a dead stop. This will catch the dust in the duster, preventing the dust from flying around the room. Continue the same method with each downward stroke. Take the duster outside and shake well. Turn your miniblind slats the opposite way and dust the front in the same long, slow strokes, stopping at the bottom.

Should your mini-blinds be very dirty or greasy, you may need to remove them from the brackets and wash them in the bathtub with hot, sudsy water. Put a tablespoon of automatic dishwasher powder in the water and they will dry as the water sheets off.

You can also take the mini-blinds outside and hose them off using a soft brush or cloth and a bucket of water with the dishwasher powder. Once sparkling clean, maintain them with your feather duster twice a month. It will take such little time.

You can use your feather duster on the TV, VCR, picture frames, windowsills, etc. Don't forget to use slow strokes, stopping at the end, then shaking outside to remove dust from Mr. Feather Duster.

Your pumice stone (hardware and beauty supply stores have them) gets the ugly ring out of the toilet bowl caused by rust and mineral deposits. It is amazing how fast it will remove the scale. Just rub it on the ring gently and it's gone. It will also clean ovens. It removes carbon buildup on grills, and iron cookware, paint from concrete and masonry walls, plus scales from swimming pools.

Your old toothbrush will clean hard-to-get-to corners of the shower floors, and around faucets and sinks. The tough stuff can be gently scraped with a razor blade.

Ammonia (not the sudsy type) is good on all kitchen floors and tile.

A good trick to remember is to vacuum windowsills, windowpanes, and cross frames on the windows before cleaning your windows. Again, you can use Mr. Feather Duster. I use straight rubbing alcohol in a spray bottle for my windows and a soft, 100-percent cotton cloth—or better yet, a squeegee. When cleaning the outside, wipe top to bottom, and clean the inside left to right. Should you miss a spot, you'll quickly know what side you missed.

Get out the hair dryer and use it to blow the dust off silk flowers. Preferably go outside to do this with a long extension cord on the hair dryer. If the flowers are not too dusty and just need to be maintained, use the feather duster.

Remember to change your heat and air-conditioner filters at least once a year and, better yet, twice a year. This will prevent black soot from staining your walls and ceilings at the air vents. The only cleaning needed will be the feather duster.

Mr. Feather Duster will help also in these most-overlooked areas: drapes at the top, the television picture tube, and rungs or crossbars on chairs and tables. Clean your telephones with your spray bottle of rubbing alcohol and your cotton cloth. Light bulbs on table lamps, the inside surface of lamp shades, baseboards, chandelier chains, fan blades of ceiling and window fans, tops of bookshelves, and areas around your electrical cords that collect floor dust are all areas that should not be forgotten.

Anytime you clean a bookshelf or the shelves in your refrigerator, use the left-to-right method. There's no need to take everything out—merely move all items to the right and clean and then shift to the left, clean, and relocate items. Remember to clean from top to bottom. Use a spray cleaner—it's easy to apply and wipe dry. If your shelves are too full, then remove only enough so you can move the rest from side to side. Drawers and bins in the refrigerator should be removed so they can be cleaned inside and out. Be sure to catch the area under the bottom drawers. Water and gunk accumulate there.

I also use lazy Susans in my refrigerator for juice, milk, salad dressings, etc. These can be twirled around so any item is reachable from the front. Many times this will avoid a nasty spill by children reaching to the back and accidently dumping milk on the floor.

GET ORGANIZED

There may be nothing wrong with you,
The way you live, the work you do,
But I can very plainly see
Exactly what is wrong with me.
It isn't that I'm indolent;
I work as hard as anyone,
And yet I get so little done,
The morning goes, the noon is here,
Before I know, the night is near,
And all around me, I regret,
Are things I haven't finished yet.
If I could just get organized!
I often times have realized
Not all that matters is the man;
The man must also have a plan.

With you, there may be nothing wrong,
But here's my trouble right along;
I do the things that don't amount
To very much, of no account,
That really seem important though
And let a lot of matters go.
I nibble this, I nibble that,
But never finish what I'm at,
I work as hard as anyone,
And yet, I get so little done,
I'd do so much you'd be surprised,
If I could just get organized!

—Douglas Malloch

When we *care* for our homes, it will bring a great feeling of accomplishment. Our belongings will last longer, and we can maintain our homes so they look pretty and clean most of the time. Those drop-in visitors will not send us scurrying around to clean up. We'll feel proud to have family and guests arrive anytime.

Hospitality begins by caring to clean. Put on a pot of water for tea, pick or buy a few fresh flowers for your spanking-clean home, and enjoy the blessings of it and the family God has given you.

Do it! Do it right! Do it now!

SHE'S ORGANIZED

She rises early, near dawn
    to begin a new day
And spends time with the Lord
    to start the right way.
        She's organized....

Breakfast is ready, lunches complete.
    Now time to wake
Everyone else from their sleep.
        She's organized....

Out the door all must go
   to their respective places.
She leaves each with a kiss
   and smiles on their faces.
     She's organized....

Dishes are finished, first load of wash done.
   Floors are all vacuumed.
Dusting is done.
     She's organized....

Monday's chores are completed, so the 3x5 says,
   Now for marketing and shopping
And lunch with a friend.
     She's organized....

She's turned cleaning and planning
   into a full-time career;
Speaking to ladies and church groups,
   some far and some near.
     She's organized....

Hubby Bob is the man behind what you see,
   Keeping "More Hours in My Day" a reality.
He boxes and ships many items per week,
   and keeps things running smooth—that's his
   specialty,
     He's organized....

What a team they've become,
   both at home and away;
Helping others like us have more time in our day!

                —Sheri Torelli

TOTAL MESS TO TOTAL REST CHART
Suggested Areas To Clean

D = Daily	Q = Quarterly
EOD = Every Other Day	Y = Yearly
W = Weekly	Bi = Twice a Year
M = Monthly	

❀ KITCHEN	Freq.	Est. Time		Freq.	Est. Time
Dishes			Clean cupboard drawers		
Wash dishes	D	10mi	Clean window over sink		
Dry dishes, put away			Wash countertops		
Fill dishwasher	D		Wash canisters		
Empty dishwasher	D		Clean knickknacks		
Clean dishwasher door	W	1mi	Wash/polish woodwork		
Wash pots/pans			Clean fan		
Scour sinks			Walls/ceiling; Paint/wash		
Polish fixtures			Wash/dry-clean curtains		
Floors			Clean toaster/can opener		
Sweep/damp-mop floor	EOD		Clean cutting board		
Wash floor			Empty garbage		
Wax floor	Q	10mi	Clean light fixtures	Bi	30mi
Strip old wax	Y	1hr	Clean telephone	M	2mi
Shake scatter rugs			Clean ceiling fans	Q	4mi
Vacuum kitchen carpet					
Shampoo kitchen carpet					
Range/Oven					
Scour/replace drip pans			❀ BATHROOM ☐1 ☑2 ☐ ☐		
Cover drip pans in foil			Clean tub	EOD	2mi
Scour rims			Clean sink	EOD	1mi
Clean under drip pans			Clean toilet	W	2mi
Clean knobs/clock			Clean shower stall	W	3mi
Clean range hood			Wash shower door/curtain	M	3mi
Clean oven inside/outside			Wash scatter rugs	Q	30mi
Microwave inside/outside			Wash/dry-clean curtains		
Refrigerator/Freezer			Clean out medicine cabinet		
Defrost freezer	Bi		Wash mirror		
Clean inside/outside/top	M	10mi	Wash walls/ceiling (paint)		
Clean drip pan	Q	2mi	Clean/polish tile		
Cupboards/Drawers			Clean mini-blinds		
Under sink					
Empty/wash shelves					
Dump anything dead					
Change shelf paper					

TOTAL MESS TO TOTAL REST CHART

	Freq.	Est. Time		Freq.	Est. Time
❁ BATHROOM CONTINUED			Clean mirrors		
Floors			Dust lamp shades		
Wash floor			Move furniture to clean		
Wax floor			Wash walls		
Strip old wax			Paint walls		
Vacuum carpet			Remove cobwebs		
Shampoo carpet			Clean furnace vents		
Cupboards/Drawers			Change furnace filter		
Clean/organize			Change air conditioner filter		
Clean/polish woodwork					
Polish countertops			**❁ LAUNDRY**		
Clean brushes/combs			Wash/dry		
			Fold/put away		
❁ BEDROOMS 1 2 3 4 ☐			Mend/iron		
Make bed	D	2mi	Do hand washables		
Turn mattress	Bi	2mi			
Wash mattress pad/bedding	Q	30mi	**❁ PET CARE**		
Clean under bed	M	2mi	Bathe dog	Q	15mi
Vacuum	W	5mi	Change kitty litter	W	3mi
Polish furniture	W	5mi	Clean bird/hamster cage	W	4mi
Dust furniture	W	5mi			
Dust picture frames	M	1mi	**❁ MISCELLANEOUS**		
Clean closets/drawers	Q	6mi	Prepare meals		
Wash window (inside)			Set table		
Wash blinds			Polish shoes		
Clean mirrors	M	4mi	Bake		
			Change sheets		
			Water plants		
❁ LIVING ROOM /FAMILY ROOM			Clean fingerprints from walls		
Vacuum carpet			Clean light switches		
Shampoo carpet			Dust high places/ledges		
Dust furniture			Clean purse		
Polish furniture			Sort seasonal clothing		
Clean fireplace			Clean out car		
Window (inside)			Wash car		
Dust picture frames			Polish/wash purses		
Wash ornaments					
Wash/dry-clean drapes					

TOTAL MESS TO TOTAL REST CHART

	Freq.	Est. Time		Freq.	Est. Time
❀ OUTDOORS			Read		
Sweep patio	W	5mi	Study	D	30mi
Sweep porch/walks	W	5mi	Fun shopping	D	30mi
Mow lawn	W	30mi	Lunch out	W	1hr
Do gardening	W	1hr	Hobbies/sewing/crafts		
Clean up leaves	W	15mi	**❀ EXERCISE**		
Do pruning	Bi	1hr	Jog		
Wash windows (outside)	Q	2hr	Walk		
❀ SPECIAL PROJECTS			Tennis		
Plan vacations/birthdays					
Plan Christmas			**❀ CLASSES**		
Write letters			Bible study	W	1hr
Sew			Women's ministries		
❀ FAMILY			**❀ PERSONAL GROOMING**		
Family Counsel			Shower		
Dinner/breakfast out			Shampoo		
Fun activities with children			Makeup (one card)		
Church			Shave legs/underarms		
Children's lessons			Manicure		
Candlelight dinner			Pedicure		
Love basket			Haircut	M	1hr.
			Permanent	Q	2hr
❀ FINANCE					
Balance checkbook	M	30mi	**❀ VISITING**		
Do bookkeeping/budget			Friends		
			The elderly		
❀ PERSONAL ACTIVITIES			Shut-ins		
Bible reading	D	10mi	Telephoning		
Prayer	D	10mi	**❀ ERRANDS**		
Doctor			Banking		
Dentist	Bi	1hr	Dry cleaners		
Church			Return recyclables		
Choir			Post Office		
Sunday School			Grocery shopping	W	1hr
Meetings			**❀ HOME ORGANIZATION**		
Youth Group			Menu planning/check freezer		
Bible study			Compile grocery list		

6 | Caring Through Eliminating Home Messies

♥

No form of society can be reasonably stable in which the majority of the people are not fairly content. People cannot be content if they feel that the foundations of their lives are wholly unstable.

—James Truslow Adams

AS I SPEAK AROUND the country, I have found that when you have a mess organizationally, everything in your physical environment and how it's organized, managed, and maintained holds you at your current level of effectiveness. When you're overwhelmed, you can't see anything else. You can't see new opportunities, challenges, or even how to care for another person. It's like, "Are you kidding? I've got too much to handle already."

I tell the ladies at our seminars to say "no" to good things and save their "yes" for the best. A lot of us are overcommitted and need to clean out the messies in our lives that won't let us take on better activities.

The messies in the home many times reflect messies in someone's personal life. My book *Survival for Busy Women*[1] goes into great detail showing how you can establish lifetime goals and theme verses. If you don't know what you want out of life, it's hard to prioritize the activities of your life. Taking the time to establish goals for our lives is very basic to helping us clean out the messies that prevent us from doing the things we want to do, but don't have time to do.

There are basic questions that we women need to ask ourselves as we prepare to eliminate the mess and clutter from our lives.

- Who are you?
- Where are you going?
- What do you need to get there?
- Does this make you money?
- Does this save you money?
- Does this save you time?
- Does this improve the quality of your life?

These are some very penetrating philosophical and theological questions—tough questions and answers that we must deal with before we begin tossing things out of our lives. You might be asking yourself, "I didn't want to get this complicated. I just wanted to get rid of my messies so I could give more time to caring for other ladies." You may want to *care*, but God might want you to come to grips with who you are first.

What most of us need is to live in a state of contentment. In Philippians 4:11 Paul reminds us to be content in whatever state we find ourselves. One of the by-products of our Western culture is people who are not content with their jobs, husbands, children, churches, homes, clothes, food, freeways, and life in general. We are a society of malcontents just waiting for retirement or the rapture, whichever comes first.

Thomas Fuller states, "Contentment consists not in adding more fuel, but in taking away some fire; not in multiplying of wealth, but in subtracting men's desires."[2] I have a motto: "Less is best." When you don't have something, you don't have to dust it, paint it, repair it, or replace it. When we are young, we strive to consume, and as we get older we try to cut back and eliminate those possessions from our lives which rob us of being content. When we can't find contentment within ourselves, it is useless to seek it elsewhere. It's not there! You choose to be "content" or "discontent." Which will it be? Whichever option you choose will determine if you are ready to eliminate the messies and clutter from your life, home, and work.

As long as you choose "discontent," you will have clutter in your personal affairs. Only when you get right with God and find His plan for your life will you be able to muster up the desire and discipline to make a new *you*! "Major on the major and minor on the minor" and "first things first" are both good slogans to help us understand what needs to be done.

After you come to grips with who you are and why you are here, you are ready to eliminate some of the time and money robbers from your home. As you go through some of these areas, you will be amazed at how this process will change your life. These basic questions are not found in pill form but are lifetime pursuits in growing into the woman that God wants you to become.

Several of the letters I have received lately will give you encouragement:

———————— ♥ ————————

Dear Emilie,

I'm writing this note to express my gratitude for your books *More Hours in My Day* and *Survival for Busy Women*. They have been lifesavers for me!

I am a student (I plan to become a teacher) and was married early this year. My husband and I are delighted to be expecting our first child late this fall. Since money has been tight, I have been working outside the home. With the wedding expenses and all, we really needed as much as I could bring in. Juggling school, work, and fighting fatigue from pregnancy has left my home a disaster zone. My husband is lucky if I can hustle up enough energy to iron a clean shirt for him each morning. We are both Christians and he is a traditional man (i.e., he does yard work and hopes to have the inside of the house relatively clean). Even though he doesn't ask for much, I have not been able to keep organized. We have come to the end of our rope and a decision (my decision) was made today. I've decided that my home/husband comes first. I plan to quit work as soon as they find a replacement. My husband says it doesn't matter to him. What does matter is that I am happy and am not sad to be around all the time. Now I am excited that I can implement all of the good advice and the program from *More Hours in My Day* and get my home organized. I can't tell you what a relief this is. I honestly don't think I would have even thought about home management as a priority in my life if it had not been for your books! God Bless!

—Kathy Davis
Southern California

———————— ♥ ————————

Dear Emilie,

I have never told you what your ministry means to me. When I first heard you speak about your children and your brother's children, you were a light at the end of the tunnel. I had a 5- and 4-year-old, plus an 8-year-old. Having children 14 months apart, I didn't go anywhere for 3 years! I wasn't organized. My mother had to work when I was growing up. The only thing she taught me was guilt over not turning my mattress in the spring.

I thank you for sharing your life with us. You are a blessing. Thanks for everything!

—Debbie Thompson
Southern California

——————— ♥ ———————

Dear Mrs. Barnes,

I want to personally thank you for writing two books, *More Hours in My Day* and *Survival for Busy Women*. I purchased them about a year ago and started trying to put a few of your ideas into practice. They worked for a while, but soon all the best-laid plans failed. I felt hopeless. My whole house seemed to mount up against me! It seemed I was destined to be a sloppy housekeeper and mother.

While we were on vacation I took your two books with me to reread and rethink what I did wrong. I figured if this lady with five young children could keep order in the Barnes' home, surely I ought to be able to keep order in the Suggs' home with only two children. So I delved into the books looking for clues. Then the Holy Spirit pricked my heart. He showed me my biggest mistake was not giving God the proper place in my life. I was a Christian, but I had gotten slack the last couple of years in prayer, Bible study, and just plain time to meditate on God.

That night I sat up after everyone went to bed and wrote out my prayer to God, then waited for Him to give me some direction on which way to go. Funny, His answers were not much different from the original, but they were in different order and from a whole new perspective.

Since I've been home, I've put my new priorities into practice. So far they have worked great. Even better than expected!

I've begun keeping a preschool little girl so a good friend could return to school, and I've still been able to maintain my household. I've also been nominated for Preschool Director at my church (something I hadn't planned on happening for for several more years on my old priority list). The list could go on and on and there are still areas to be worked on.

I know God deserves all the glory, but I wanted to thank His instrument for helping me open my eyes *to a better way of life*!

—Cora Suggs
Alabama

———— ♥ ————

Dear Emilie,

I just want you to know how much it has helped me to read your book *Survival for Busy Women*. I've read time management, home management, and self-management books before and, to be honest, I always thought they were silly and out of touch with the real world. But yours is so helpful and sensible. In fact, my husband has accused me of being stricken with a bizarre illness that makes me want to organize things (he's bewildered, but delighted).

One of the many reasons that working mothers so often carry around a sense of guilt and failure is that they never have time to keep their homes and lives organized the way they would like to. I think by adopting even one or two of the techniques from your book, women can feel better about themselves and relieve some of their guilt.

Congratulations on a wonderful book, and best wishes for continued success in your writing ministry.

—Elsa Houtz
Florida

———— ♥ ————

Dear Mrs. Barnes,

I am a Christian with four children (ages 5, 4, 2½, and 6 months) and a husband who works a swing shift. I bought your book *Survival for Busy Women* and enjoyed reading it. Still, I am having a somewhat difficult time applying it to my life. It seems to take every ounce of energy and every minute of the day (and night, many times) just to keep everybody clean and fed and the house from being condemned by the Board of Health. A quiet time with the Lord is becoming harder to come by all the time. The laundry, dishes, and floors (we can't afford carpet yet) are endless and, because of my husband's work, our hours are never the same.

I want to be the very *best* wife and mother possible. Do you have any tips for my situation?

I know that you're very busy and I am doubtful that you'll have time to answer my letter, but I thought I'd take a chance and write anyway. Thanks for the advice in your book.

> —Alayne McCarther
> Texas
> (resident cook, maid, nanny, mistress, accountant, nurse, etc...)

P.S. Needless to say, I do not work. I do not wish to, but it wouldn't pay to if I did.

───────── ♥ ─────────

Dear Emilie,

I have only been a homemaker for 1½ years, give or take a few months either way. My husband and I were married 20 months ago and I left my comfortable Pennsylvania home of 23 years to travel across the country with my U.S.M.C. husband. Over five months ago he left with his unit to be stationed in Japan. I was not allowed to go with him. A week after he left, you visited my church, St. Francis Catholic Church in Vista, California. Another Marine Corps "widow" friend and I were greatly inspired by your seminar and our husbands have been hearing your name frequently. I had the privilege of visiting my husband since he's been gone, and I tried out some of your recipes on him, which of course he loved.

I am sending for the remaining five cookbooks which I do not have, but I have one request. I am completely out of practice in the kitchen and would appreciate receiving your books a few days before he comes home. I've got about three weeks left, so could you send these to me ASAP? I have great expectations of the results!

Thank you again for your seminar and creativity. Hope to hear from you SOON!

—Denise MacMurtrie
Southern California

———————— ♥ ————————

Dear Emilie,

I certainly have enjoyed your book *Survival for Busy Women.* I received it through information on a "Focus on the Family" broadcast. I am a full-time career woman, but we have no children yet. Still, being *very* involved musically at our Bible church (my husband is the organist, and I'm in the choir, plus do many specials) we seem to have *no* extra time! The biggest problem is leaving the house at 8:00 A.M. and not returning at all until 9:00 P.M. due to meetings and other obligations. That is my *biggest* problem. I like to be organized, but am never home to do it. A career, church, and now house-hunting is just about doing us in.

Life needs to slow down soon for us! Thanks for your encouragement!

—Connie Begly
Illinois

———————— ♥ ————————

Now that you are ready to begin you might want to design a battle plan to straighten out your messies. I would recommend that you read three of my books to help give you an overall point of view regarding organization. They are *More Hours in My Day*, *The Complete Home Organizer*, and *Survival for Busy Women*. All these books have been published by Harvest House and may be purchased at your local Christian bookstore, market display rack with other inspirational books, or ordered directly from our office. (See page 6.)

Battle Plan Projects

The motto we have in our home is "Do the worst first." In many homes that means the garage, wardrobe closets, kitchen cupboards, or just general paper messes all through the home.

I try to have several rules which I go by during this reconstruction period of my life:

- Turn on good, upbeat music.

- No telephone calls.

- No visitors unless you can recruit a friend to help you (no sanguines—they usually talk more than work).

- Have the total family help on the big projects (particularly on children's bedrooms, bathrooms, and garages).

- Concentrate on one project or area at a time.

- Don't attempt to keep everything. Some things have to go (garage sales, church, Salvation Army). Some things must succumb to the trash can.

- No TV or any other distractions.

Below you will find some tips to solve your most common messies problems.

Garage

This is usually the most difficult area to straighten out. It's too big of a project for just you. This project will test you to see how good of a recruiter you are with your husband and children. Preplan and set a date on your calendar so you can attack this monster as a team. "United we stand, divided we fall." Even if you have to bribe the family with a special trip, food, or luxury item, it's worth it.

Tools: Take a corner of the garage for the "tool center." You might need to prepurchase some pegboards with hardware, lumber for shelving, a new toolbox (try garage sales), an unpainted chest-of-drawers, or a fancy prebuilt garage organizer closet. (Check your local newspaper or telephone Yellow Pages.) It may not be perfect, but at least you will have your tools in one central area so you can find the hammer, saw, pliers, and nails.

Auto supplies: Plastic dishpan-type bins or plastic potato storage bins are wonderful for storing all the waxes, cleaners, rags, and toothbrushes you use in keeping your car clean. Remember: You feel better as a person when your car is clean. We keep our safety supplies in the trunk of our car. Things like jumper cables, flares, rags, window scrapers, fire extinguisher, basic repair tools, a flashlight with extra batteries, and a pair of work gloves really come in handy when we need them.

Magazines: It's amazing how magazines are attracted to a corner of that crowded garage. Remember the magazine with the patio you planned to build, the new recipe for that yummy lemon cake, the new fabric for the couch—but *do* you remember which one? Of course not, but it's there someplace. Go through each old magazine and cut out any articles you must read. I staple them together and place them in my "To read" folder or in my manila file folders which are labeled: food, insurance, patios, decks, insurance, etc. Then throw the rest of the magazines out for the trash man. You might run across some special articles that some of your friends might enjoy. Just jot little messages on Post-it notes and send the articles off to them. They will be so impressed that you thought of them. The next time you go someplace where you will have to wait, take that "To Read" folder along with you so you can catch up on the reading. In the future, tear out the articles from your magazine when you are finished with them and file the articles away—no more stacks of magazines to clutter the garage.

Hardware: Plastic and glass jars can be used to store all those little items that we don't know what to do with: nails, tacks, screws, molly bolts, etc. You can store the jars on the shelves you installed. Screw or nail jar lids to the underside of the shelves, and simply screw and unscrew the jar rather than the lids. Clear jars let you see the contents easily and save time from looking at what's inside the jars.

Bicycles: Get some large-size J-hooks (found at hardware stores) and screw them into the underside of a 2″ x 6″ rafter. Turn your bicycle upside down and put the hooks through the spokes of your tires and lower the bicycle so the tires cradle into the J-hooks. This will really give you a lot of extra storage space.

Gardening tools: No need to keep having that rake, hoe, shovel, and edger fall against the automobile paint job. Two helpful hints are to 1) Nail a 2″ x 4″ or 2″ x 6″ stud horizontally at about 6-foot height along one of the walls, preferably near the opening of the garage so you can save steps when you are working in the yard. (The hardware store has ready-made hardware for those garden-tool handles. The hardware is easy to install too.) 2) Purchase a 30-gallon trash can and turn the handles of your tools upside down and place them into the trash can. This takes up little space in the garage and you can see the tool you need very easily. If you have a lot of gardening tools, you may want to place some weight in the bottom of the trash can so it won't tip over.

Leaf blower: Buy that inexpensive leaf blower (wait until it's on sale or at a garage sale) with a 50-to-100-foot extension cord. It makes a fast way to blow out the garage when it's dirty. In just 3-5 minutes you are finished. It even gets behind those little crevices that a broom can't reach. It's also a good way to blow clear the patio, front walkway, and back porch (much faster than a broom). It's even great for leaves.

Closets

I recommend that you take everything out of the closets and start all over. Vacuum them out and wipe down the walls, floors, and shelves. On occasion a new paint job will freshen up the areas.

Hall Closets: Eliminate everything that doesn't belong there: clothes that don't fit or aren't in style, sports items that need to be put someplace else, etc. Give yourself a real thrill and purchase some of those new colored plastic hangers. The uniformity will not only give you more space, but it will also make you feel better. Put back only those items that belong there. Remember to save room for a few extra blank hangers for your guests when they visit and need to hang up a coat or sweater.

Wardrobe closets: In our wardrobe closets we usually have three sizes of clothes:

- The size you used to wear
- The size you hope to wear
- The size you actually wear.

Determine where you are size-wise and reorganize the other sizes someplace else. Some clothes can be given to a friend who wears your old size. Seasonal clothes should be rotated between your bedroom closet and another wardrobe closet in the home. If you don't have one, you can purchase an inexpensive one to place out in the garage. They come in flexible styles for standing or hanging—whichever fits your needs. In our home we have a motto that helps prevent stuffing new clothes into the closet: *"When something new comes in, something old goes out."* That goes for underwear, hosiery, ties, nightgowns, slippers, shoes, etc. Too many is too many!

The new-style wardrobe organizers that you see advertised on TV, radio, or local newspapers are great additions to your home. You will be amazed at how much more space you have. You can even find space to get those shoes off the floor. Also, you don't need a small ladder to get things off that top shelf. There is no more top shelf, but you do have added space you can reach. With this new addition, a new paint job will really set it off. Then you can stand back, stretch your arms, and say, "Well done. I really feel good."

Bathrooms

Here is an area where the children can be a great help. I highly recommend that you let your children be a part of revamping their areas of responsibility. If they help solve the problem, they are more apt to keep the area straightened up. Evaluate each bathroom to see:

- Do I need more cupboard space?
- Do I need more shelving?
- Do I need some cleaning materials?
- Do I need some towel bars or rings?
- Could I use new paint, wallpaper, towels, and floor mats?

After inventorying your needs, take your children with you to help solve the problems. Maybe a portable shelf or rack that loops over the shower head to hold shampoo supplies will help. A tub tray also helps in storing bath toys, soap, brushes, and sponges. Lazy Susans are one of my favorite tools under the bathroom sinks. They spin around and you can pull out the bottles and jars without knocking over the ones next to them. Wicker divider trays help separate cosmetics, Q-tips, hair spray, perfume, nail clippers, etc. You can even get them covered with fabric to match the decor of your bathroom. After this rehabilitation project, the children will say, "Thanks, Mom. Now I can find my things and hang up things that have been on the floor before. I feel so special." The new look will make them proud of their room.

"Responsibility comes easier with pride."

Kitchen

The kitchen benefits from periodic cleaning. Reorganizing the refrigerator, pantry, and freezer can also be an economical way to use up forgotten stored foods. Some ideas to help in this area include:

- Start with the freezer compartment of the refrigerator. Discard old, frozen-over goods. Defrost if necessary and make a plan to consume items that have been around for awhile. I recommend that you date each item when you put it in the freezer and take time to list what is in your surprise package. I have found that Tupperware and Rubbermaid have some excellent clear containers for easy viewing. Even with those containers I still write what's in them. Foods change looks when they are frozen. Many times these surprises make an excellent soup mix. The children will say, "Mom, this is so good. You are so creative."

- Cleaning out the refrigerator is done more often because the foods let you know when they are rotten. Discard mayonnaise or salad dressing if the oil has separated or if it looks or smells odd. Mold can be cut off hard cheese and scraped off jelly if you take an extra scoop off for safety. Discard moldy bread, pastry, soft foods, or liquids. If in doubt, it's best to discard where children or animals won't find the food and eat it.

- If you store canisters of flour, sugar, meal, tea, grains, and coffee on the countertop, remember to move them and clean under and alongside them. In a tight-lidded canister, sugar will keep up to two years. Flour should last six to eight months. Take a close look at grain and pasta products and discard any that contain weevils or other bugs. In an airtight container, tea bags maintain good quality for about 18 months. Unopened ground coffee in a can lasts two years. Once open, coffee loses its flavor rapidly.

- If your spices are stored above the range, it would be better to find another place. The heat and humidity drive the flavor out. Lazy Susans in a pantry are a great place to easily store these spices.

- Pantries have a way of collecting all kinds of food. Many canned items will last three to five years provided the can is not bulging, leaking, or dented. Quality may decline with age. Boxed spaghetti and other pasta should last a year or more, as do dry cake mixes. Some packages have "use by" dates which should be checked during the cleaning process. Discard those that have expired. Home-canned items should be used within a year. Never taste suspicious-looking-or-smelling canned goods or anything that spurts liquid when opened.

The U.S. Department of Agriculture maintains a toll-free telephone number staffed by trained home economists who can answer food storage questions. Call (800) 535-4555 weekdays.

Junk Drawers: Our new daughter-in-law, Maria, looked into our junk drawer the other evening and said, "That's the best-organized junk drawer I have ever seen." Where do we put all those rubber bands, paper clips, old keys, matchbooks, mismatched screws and bolts, and next spring's garden seeds? You can purchase at your local kitchen supply store some plastic organizational trays that fit into the bottom of the drawer. I choose ones that have openings in the bottom of the tray. This lets the crumbs and dirt fall through the trays into the drawer bottom. It's easier to clean the drawer this way. Just lift out the tray and wipe the bottom of the drawer. Old egg cartons also make excellent trays and compartments for storing all that junk. They are also inexpensive.

Some helpful hints for your kitchen are:

- Place the plastic lids from coffee cans under bottles of cooking oil to keep cabinets clean. When the lids get dirty, just throw them away.

- A rubber jar opener (or rubber gloves) gives you easy access to anything in a tightly closed jar.

- To cover kitchen cabinet shelves, I apply easy-to-install vinyl floor squares by just peeling off the backing. They are particularly good for lower shelves where pots and pans are usually stored. They cut easily and do not tear or wrinkle.

- One of the best appliances I have for my busy schedule is my Crockpot. I prepare the meal early in the morning and when I come home from shopping or work, I find our main dish for dinner ready.

- At least once a year pull the plug on your refrigerator and give it a thorough cleaning. Rinse with clean water after cleaning with baking soda (one Tbsp. of baking soda to one quart of water). Let it air dry.

- A trash can under the kitchen sink takes up some very valuable storage space. We take a large, decorative basket and line it with a plastic bag. The bag is easy to lift out when full. Train several family members to help take the trash out.

- To avoid a smelly garbage disposal, run cold water and the disposal at the same time for a while with each use of the disposal. Lemon peel will also freshen up the disposal. Drop it in and turn on the disposal with the water running.

- To speed up a sluggish drain, first run hot tap water down the drain, then pour in three tablespoons of baking soda and one-half cup of distilled white vinegar. Stop up the drain and wait 15 minutes. The baking soda and vinegar will foam up, reacting with each other, and will eat away at whatever is slowing the drain. Finally, flush the drain with hot tap water.

- Have fresh lemon juice all year long. Squeeze lemons and freeze the juice in ice cube trays. Transfer the frozen cubes into freezer bags. Defrost for fresh lemon juice anytime.

- Use pressure cookers, microwave ovens, or electric pans or ovens when you can. They use less energy than your stove or oven.

- Do not store cookies, cereal, or other "bait" by the stove. Children can get burned climbing on the stove to reach an item overhead.

- Use glass or ceramic pans for baking; you can reduce your oven temperature by 25°.

- Instead of using the dry cycle on your dishwasher, open the machine and pull out the top shelf just an inch or so to prop the door slightly open. The escaping steam helps to dry the dishes almost as well as the dry cycle. It's much faster, and it saves energy and money.

- I've found an easy way to clean the grater: Before using it, spray with no-stick vegetable spray.

- Want spotless dishes whenever you use the dishwasher? Then be careful at the supermarket. Shake the box of dishwasher detergent; it should sound loose and powdery. Old, lumpy detergent won't do the job properly.

- Line the bottom of the sink with a towel when you wash your precious glassware or fragile ceramic plates.

- A great way to repair those nicks on your kitchen cabinets: Go over the nicks with a marker that matches the finish of the cabinets. You can polish over them with clear fingernail polish.

Laundry

Too often we let this area get totally out of hand: piles of dirty clothes, clothes that need repair, clothes that need to be ironed. How in the world do we get on top of this mountain of mess? In my previously recommended books, I go to great detail in giving many ideas on how to conquer this demon. You might want to refer to these books for more details. Here are some immediate hints to get you started:

- Use three large containers or three pillow-sized bags that hang from hooks to sort your dirty clothes: one for whites, one for darks, and one for mixed colors. Even children at a very young age can help sort dirty clothes this way.

- Use a special basket for repairs where you can place any clothes that need a button, a mend, or an alteration.

- To cut down on ironing time, put a rack or stand near the dryer and hang clothes on hangers as soon as the machine stops.

- Buy clothes that don't need ironing. Wash-and-wear clothing really cuts down on ironing time.

- If you are tired of your box of laundry soap taking up so much room, you can take an old canister and fill it up with your favorite detergent and you will have more room.

- When your iron sticks, just sprinkle a little salt onto a piece of waxed paper and run the hot iron over it. Rough, sticky spots will disappear as if by magic.

- When I want to wash a rug that sheds, I put it in a pillowcase (an old one that I keep just for that purpose) and tie the top well. Then I have no mess in the washer. Just shake out the pillowcase.

- If starch sticks to the bottom of your iron, scour it with steel wool. Never scratch it off with a knife or a razor blade.

- Ironing boards never seem to have enough padding. When the pad on your ironing board is ready to be thrown out, leave the pad on the board. Just add your new pad and cover up the old one.

- Metal zippers work more smoothly when you occasionally rub the teeth with a bit of wax or bar of soap.

- To freshen laundry, add one-third cup of baking soda to the wash or rinse cycle. Clothes will smell sweeter and cleaner.

- Stack towels, washcloths, and linens with the folded edge toward you. This makes it easy to pick up one at a time when you reach for them on the shelf.

- Always wash knitwear inside out when washing either by hand or machine to avoid snags.

- Don't overload your washing machine. This turns out a poor wash.

- To make your blankets fluffier, add two cups of white vinegar to a washer tub of rinse water.

- Hang a whisk broom on a hook beneath your ironing board. Use it to remove lint when pressing clothes.

- Use warm water to sprinkle your clothes. It penetrates them better. Allow clothes to absorb the moisture at least three hours before ironing.

Paper

One of the hardest projects in getting back on track is what to do with all your paper. Paper paralysis is one of the most difficult procrastinations to get a move on. Our motto is *"Don't put it down—put it away."* In order to put it away, you must have a plan for all that paper. I recommend different-colored file folders with these headings:

- To read
- To do
- For Bob
- To pay
- To file
- Junk mail

To read: All the personal letters and magazines I put in this folder to get to at night when I'm in bed. This is a good time to go through this stack of paper since there's no pressure and it's at the end of the day. I also grab this folder if I'm going someplace where I might have to wait.

To do: In this folder, I put all of my follow-up paper: letters to be answered, projects to be completed, reports to be made, and follow-up items with due dates. If there are urgent due dates, I will note these on my monthly calendar in my notebook and highlight them in red so they catch my eye.

For Bob: Much of the paper that comes in is for my husband. I place all of his paper in his special folder and give it to him on a regular basis. When he was in business, his folder was placed where he would see it when he came home in the evening. Now that we are working together in our ministry, he gets the folder on a regular basis each day—usually right after the mail comes in.

To pay: House payments, medical bills, taxes, insurance, etc. all go in this folder for future payment. During the last week of the month I pull out this folder and sit down at my desk to write checks to cover these bills. Bob pays all bills regarding our ministry. If any of those bills come in the mail, I put them in Bob's folder and he pays those invoices from our ministry account.

To file: When all the papers have been processed and need to be filed, I put them in this folder and, on a regular basis (once or twice a week), I take this folder with me to the three-drawer file cabinets and file items into the pertinent file-folder headings. I forward all income, state, and federal tax-related papers to Bob for filing. He in turn files these papers away until tax time, then he retrieves and summarizes all data for our certified public accountant.

Junk mail: This is my first "folder"—usually the trash can. I keep very little junk mail, and I get this off my desk immediately. If anything catches my eye, I put them in my "To read" folder for more in-depth study. Don't get bogged down with junk mail. It warrants very low priority.

Photographs

"I know those pictures we took at the beach last summer are in this pile of pictures. I sure wish there was an easy way to find them." There are several good storage ideas on the market. Whichever system you use, you must process photos immediately or you will become stressed out and find yourself under the photo pile again. Use the simplest method. I have three parts to my system: photo albums, plastic file boxes, and shoeboxes for negatives.

Photo albums: I have several albums of different people in our family:

- A general catchall album.
- Separate albums for our children, Jenny and Brad.
- Separate albums for our three grandchildren: Christine, Chad, and Bevan.

When a roll of film gets developed, I decide if I want to place any of these photos in my albums or if I want to keep them loose and file them in my plastic file box. Our market prints two pictures for the price of one, and I give these extras to other members of our family and also insert photos in letters to friends we don't often see. They love receiving a picture with the letter.

Our grandchildren just love to pull down their albums and see the many pictures we have of them. Often they will ask, "Grammy Em, please tell me about this picture."

If a picture isn't good or worthy to keep, I just throw it away. Not every picture is good, and we shouldn't feel guilty if we don't keep them.

Plastic file boxes: In these boxes I have used tabs to break the pictures into subject headings like adventure groups, vacations, animals, church outings, remodeling, Christmas pictures (by year), Hawaii, Mexico, Europe, etc. It is very easy for me to file any worthy pictures into their proper headings. Again, you don't have to keep every picture. It's also easy to add a new subject heading, if needed.

Shoeboxes for negatives: I take a legal-sized envelope and place my latest negatives into it and write the date these pictures were taken. In the upper right-hand corner of the envelope I write out what the pictures were about: family Christmas party 1989, Chad's first tooth, our trip to the snow at Lake Arrowhead, etc. Then I file the envelope in front of the other envelopes. Everything is filed by date and a general idea of what's included. This makes negative retrieval very easy. Again, save only those negatives you treasure. General negatives of little replacement value I don't keep. If I get a real treasure of a negative, I store it in a special envelope in our safe-deposit box at the bank. These are rare, but we do have a few stored away.

Sewing and Craft Supplies

If you can locate a special corner or space for your sewing or craft center, you are fortunate. Many people have special rooms just for this activity, but most of us are fortunate if we can allocate a closet, shelf, or pull-out cart to house this activity. If you don't have a room or free corner, use my "perfect boxes" (see page 6 for ordering information), individual plastic colored baskets, or a rolling cart with baskets to hold supplies and unfinished projects. These can be pulled out and rolled wherever you need them. Keep thread, needles, measuring tape and any other small items in tool boxes, egg cartons, plastic gadget trays, or a chest of drawers (and be sure to label each drawer). Coffee cans or oatmeal cartons can hold knitting needles. You may use a wicker basket or caddy to hold your materials for easy transport to the work area. My mother-in-law keeps all of her materials and supplies next to her TV chair so she doesn't have to make a special trip to get them. They are readily available when she wants to work on her knitting projects. Don't hang on indefinitely to small, useless scraps of material and thread. A lady attending one of my seminars told me she helped clean out her father's home after he passed away and she found a box labeled: "String too short to use." When she opened it, she found string that was too short to use. With no hesitation, she threw that box into the trash. We want to eliminate that type of storage. Some other helpful hints are:

- Crochet together those scraps of yarn to make a unique spread or afghan.

- If you have needlework patterns that become frayed because they are loose, try inserting them in 8″ x 10″ plastic refill pages for photo albums. You can read through the plastic, and the pattern won't tatter and tear.

- I keep an old jar in the wastebasket by my sewing machine. The lid has a small hole and a slot in it. When I have a dull or broken needle, I put it in this jar. I also put old razor blades in this jar. When full, I dump the jar in the trash and eliminate possible injuries.

- When sewing, drop scraps and threads into a grocery bag as you go. Don't let them clutter your machine and work area.

- I keep an up-to-date list of all my fabrics posted by my sewing area. These are organized into seasons and garments. I always read this list over before going shopping. This helps me keep impulse buying of fabrics to a minimum.

- A sewing trick I find very helpful is to cut out several dresses or items at one time and stack them by my sewing machine. Then I can sew them up when I have little bits and pieces of extra time.

- When sewing, I stitch as much together as possible on a garment before I do any ironing. For example, I stitch the darts, pockets, and all other pieces I can sew without crossing a seam. I then iron the garment and proceed.

- An easy way to thread a needle is to spray some hair spray or spray starch on your fingers and apply it to the end of the thread. The thread stiffens just enough to ease the job of guiding it through the eye of the needle.

- Keep a small magnet in your sewing basket and use it to pick up pins and needles that drop to the floor while you are sewing.

- You can reuse an old zipper by spraying it heavily with spray starch. It will sew like new.

- Here's a tip for keeping those four-hole buttons on longer: Sew through only two holes at a time, breaking the thread and knotting it for each pair of holes. This way, should one set break loose, the other side will still hold the button.

- To make additional belt holes, poke the belt with a red-hot steel knitting needle.

- A bar of soap makes an ideal place to stick needles and pins. It lubricates them so they will go through stiff fabrics with ease.

- Recycle your spotted T-shirts or blouses by decorating them with stitchery or stencils. You can create your own designer garments.

- Sewing together single or multicolored rug remnants is a task, but it does brighten up small areas of a room at a low cost.

- An easy way to hem a dress is to have a sink plunger handy to use when marking a skirt for hemming. Mark the handle at the desired length, then move the plunger around the hem. It stands by itself, leaving your hands free to mark or pin.

- After oiling your sewing machine, stitch through a blotter several times to prevent surplus oil from damaging your fabrics.

- You can sharpen a machine needle by stitching through a piece of sandpaper.

Husbands

Of all the questions I get, the most frequent is: "How do I get my husband to clean up his mess? He never throws out anything and is always collecting things. I can't live with it anymore. I want it to change, but he likes it just the way it is!" You may very well have the same comments. You are not alone in this arena.

I have found that prayer helps to change a man's heart and our impatience. I also know that a person never changes until he or she wants to change or sees a need to change. I am very fortunate in that Bob is also well-organized and he really helps me in this area. I've never had to follow behind him and pick up clothes and laundry on the floor. His mother did a good job training her boys as they were growing up.

Ladies, this is where training of our children comes in. If your children are young and still flexible in their learning habits, I really stress to teach them the basic fundamentals of home management.

Sally from a nearby city attended one of my seminars and was so challenged by this idea that she went home to her two teenage boys and designed a ten-week program based on my book *The Creative Home Organizer*. She titled it "Survival Summer." Sally took a chapter a week and stressed the fundamentals in that chapter. Her course of study was:

- Menu planning—shopping list
- Food preparation
- Laundry
- Sewing and mending
- Kitchen
- Ironing
- Housecleaning
- Basic household organization
- Basic entertaining
- Money and timesaving ideas
- Garage organization

The culminating activity was for her sons to plan, purchase, and prepare an evening meal for the family and a few invited friends. The boys did everything for the evening—even the sending out of invitations, table setting, providing the floral centerpiece, cooking the meal, and doing the dishes. Everyone gave them "A's" on their final and wanted to know when they would be doing it again.

Sally felt excited and complete as a mom. She commented to me, "Now I know they can survive if anything would happen to me." One of these days her daughters-in-law will call her blessed.

Ladies, let's not pass on another generation of ill-prepared homemakers—either sons or daughters. One of the responsibilities of being a mom (or a dad) is to train our children in the way they should go.

If all else fails with our husbands and they think the messies is all our problem, then I recommend the motto: "Yours—mine—ours."

I believe that Scripture teaches that a husband and wife should become one; however, there are times when "yours," "mine," and "ours" comes into play. Here's how it works. If your husband wants to make and live in a mess, you map out certain areas in your home that become his, and you leave those areas to him. Each husband might have certain rooms that he claims. Usually it's the garage, a workroom, and a hall closet. The "mine" area is all mine. I can keep it as tidy as I want. It might be the master bedroom, bathroom, and/or kitchen. In these areas my quest for organization comes to the forefront. No one interferes. Then there are the "ours" areas where I compromise my tidiness desires and live with a lower standard of excellence. This system is a good compromise for both husband and wife. You get a little of what you want and he can live with his desires.

This strategy works very well with teenage children, too. I've seen a lot of examples where typical sloppy teenagers have become well-organized and efficient adults.

Children

There were days when I would cry out, "If only I didn't have the children around I could keep a clean, well-organized home." Sound familiar? There is no doubt that children contribute greatly to clutter and messies. As mothers we need to be smarter than they are and figure out how they can be part of the solution.

In the previous areas I have given you some ideas on how to solicit your children's help around the home. It is amazing how plastic bins, pegs, hampers, baskets, hooks, and rolling baskets give your children resources to pick up and put away their belongings.

Last year we were in Ohio and Kentucky speaking, and we had the opportunity to visit a Shaker village that had been reconstructed to represent an early-American Shaker community. These were religious communes that came together as individuals and families to worship and farm as a way of life. As we toured the old buildings, I saw a lot of wooden pegs that were positioned about six feet off the floor. I came to learn that these pegs were there so clothes could be hung. I thought: *What a great idea!* At the souvenir shop I bought about 15 of these pegs and brought them home. I gave Bob the pegs and he took drill in hand and installed these pegs in our bedrooms. What a practical device they have been to us. Children just love them because of the ease in hanging a coat or sweater. Involve your children in deciding what they would like to do in their areas of living.

Below are some very practical ideas to use with your children:

- Have your kids used their crayons to decorate your painted walls? Try baking soda on a damp sponge to remove their murals. With a little elbow grease, your walls will look as good as new.

- Instead of a bedtime story, I tell my children the beginning of a dream and suggest they listen with their eyes closed. They are quickly sound asleep and ready to finish the dream.

- When we are dining out, these ideas help keep our children busy until the food comes: 1) Before ordering, have everyone look at the menu, point to the pictures of food and name them, and count the sandwiches or desserts and say the prices aloud. Make a list of favorite foods. 2) After deciding what to order, count how many napkins, straws, and utensils you will need. Play "Guess what's under the napkin" or "Pick up the straws." 3) Have everyone close his or her eyes and identify various sounds: people talking, a baby crying, a clock ticking, feet moving along the floor, dishes rattling. 4) Tell an add-on story: One person starts it and each person adds another sentence until your meal arrives.

• Once a year I have a baby-sitter swap party. Each attendee must bring the names and telephone numbers of three reliable sitters.

• When sewing buttons on children's clothing, use elastic thread. It makes buttoning much simpler for little fingers.

• One clever mom shared this idea: After many nights of interrupted sleep, I finally hit on a solution that keeps my five-year-old in her own bed—at least most nights. I labeled one bowl "Mama's Bed Buttons" and another "Christine's Bed Buttons" and put 25 small buttons in each. For every night Christine stays in bed, I owe her one button. She pays me a button if she gets in bed with me. When her bowl is filled with all the buttons, we do something special—a roller-skating trip, a movie, or an outing of her choice. Now she only comes to my bed if she really feels she has to.

• Here is a little idea for young children at a fast-food store or restaurant. When you buy the tot a soft drink, cut the straw off short so it is easier to hold and drink. There's less chance of a child spilling or dropping the drink, too.

• Before bed, have your family prepare everything they need for the next morning and put it on or next to the kitchen table to avoid a frantic search before you leave the house.

• To keep several kids' socks straight, assign each child a different color of sock sorters. After washing and drying, distribute socks to the owner of the appropriate color of sorters.

- Put a laundry basket in each child's room. Have each child deliver it full to the laundry room and sort the wash. Children who are tall enough to reach into the bottom of the washer can be taught how to run it.

- When I empty the dishwasher after dinner, I wrap a flatware place setting in a napkin for each family member. This way, the children are able to help set the table, and the job gets done faster.

- Children who grow up in environments full of put-downs, negative nicknames, and criticism often become critical adults. Catch your child doing something good and tell him about it. Be positive and uplifting.

- The most powerful forms of praise are given in private, one-on-one.

- The more we do for our children, the less they can do for themselves.

Now that we have established a goal and purpose for our lives and have gone through our homes to remove the piles of clutter, we are ready to branch out in caring for other people.

We are called to help others, and we need to be obedient to that call. Martin Luther stated, "How is it possible that you have not been called? You are already a married man, a wife, a child, a daughter, a servant or a maid...nobody is without command and calling.... God's eyes look not upon the works, but on the obedience in the work."[3]

——————— ♥ ———————

*Our ability to discover love will
in part depend on our ability
to handle rejection.*

7 | Things Happen When Women Care to Reach Out

———————— ♥ ————————

*T*HE FOLLOWING IS AN exciting story of what can happen when a small group of women reaches out to care for their community and the women who surround them. I received this letter in November during our very busy and heavily scheduled holiday seminar season. The letter was rather long, so I decided to set it aside until my schedule opened up a bit. This is what I read at 1:00 A.M. after a late-night drive home from a Southern California holiday seminar:

———————— ♥ ————————

Dear Emilie,

Hello! I know this holiday season is a very busy time for you, but I hope you will be able to take a few minutes to read this note and be encouraged! Three years ago I attended my first holiday seminar and I loved it! I was like a sponge soaking up all of your ideas and was highly motivated to use the creative gifts God has given to me. At the time of that holiday seminar my husband and I had just moved into a new home and new area. The Lord had spoken to us one year before that, that He was going to do a "new thing." A big part of this "new thing" in our lives involved my husband and I as lay people to stand alongside our pastor and his wife to pioneer a new church. Little did we know that the new thing God was doing in our hearts was a new love for His children in serving them and caring for them in a deeper way than we had ever experienced.

I am a mommy of three little girls and a homemaker. I love all the opportunities God has given and gives me to create atmosphere in my home and my church. I could never accomplish all God is asking me to do without becoming more organized. I'm so grateful for your wisdom and teaching tools for becoming more organized.

Our family's Scripture is also Matthew 6:33, "Seek ye first" and, although it is difficult at times in today's world to keep focused on this principle, we know in our hearts it is God's desire for us. Seeking the Lord first does require sacrifice of personal desires, finances, leisure time, etc., but what the Lord gives in return is worth more than any of those things. His blessings and promises for our girls and family are rich in peace, joy, and love. Like the Bible says, seeking Him first produces much "rich" fruit. Emilie, through your ministry many seeds have been planted in my life to help produce the fruit that God uses to touch others.

After your holiday seminar I turned to my pastor's wife and spoke out with tears that I prayed someday God would use me in a ministry such as yours. Pretty big vision I know, but over the last three years I've watched God begin to prepare me and use me in different ways on a much smaller scale. It's been exciting for me to watch God answer my prayer. Here are some of the things God has done.

Two weeks after your seminar my husband and I were presented with the opportunity to take a 17-year-old, pregnant, and unwed girl into our home. She knew the Lord, but was extremely lonely and withdrawn and hurting deeply. She spent Christmas with us. Since I had just been to your seminar, I had lots of new ideas and traditions to try. These traditions helped Khristine to probably, for the first time, experience the warmth and love that can happen to a family during the holiday season. For her, holidays had always been extremely painful and lonely due to her family circumstances. Two weeks after Christmas, Khristine's daughter, Erin, was born and they stayed with us as a family for a period of six months. That opportunity changed our lives as my husband and I saw with our eyes how painful and lonely the Christmas season can be for many people. I'm so thankful that your seminar helped to prepare me to make my home a warm and inviting place for hurting people to come. The Lord's peace is what really ministers to the hurting people that come into my home and life, but God chooses and allows me to help set a warm and loving atmosphere—what a privilege!

Last year I again was challenged by the Lord at Christmastime to open my home to the mommies and daughters from my child's classroom for a mother/daughter Christmas tea. Again, I used God's creativity in the many ideas I've received from you and provided an atmosphere where each mommy could share their heart and personal testimony of the Lord. It was a beautiful time, and I have built some wonderful relationships with those women. I have had the opportunity to teach two of the women from that tea, along with about 25 others from our church body, how to make a "care basket." This is a gift basket filled with goodies and Scriptures personalized for the person receiving the basket. I started this ministry in our church (Desert Streams Church in Canyon Country, California). It has touched hundreds of pastors and evangelists and their wives to refresh and encourage them when they come to visit our church or are on a minister's retreat.

Well, Emilie, that brings me to the last fruit I'd like to share with you that will be happening this December 2nd. "A Different Kind of Christmas" is a special outreach that the Lord birthed in the hearts of myself and a good friend, Terry. God sent us a core group of about eight women to help us with the details of this home tour where the true meaning of Christmas will be shared through testimonies of special traditions. Many other women from our church are also volunteering to help us the day of this event. I would like to personally invite you to come to our home tour. It is being held from 1:00 P.M.–4:00 P.M. Saturday, December 2, which is after your seminar at the Santa Clarita Baptist Church in Canyon Country. I would be very honored if you could come. I realize the many commitments you are already involved in during this time, so I would more than understand if you could not come.

I pray this lengthy note encourages you today with how many ways God uses your ministry to encourage others. May you be blessed for all the seeds of God's creativity and love that you are planting into women. Thank you so much for those seeds that have taken root in my life. God bless you.

—Heidi Brown

———————— ♥ ————————

Needless to say I was totally touched by Heidi's letter. At the same time, I was overwhelmed. Bob and I are so focused during this time of year ministering to hundreds of women as we jump from one church to another. To be honest, my first thought was very selfish. How could she even think we could come? But my wonderful Bob encouraged me to remember that God would make the path clear and energize us to make the effort. True, December 2 was our last seminar of the year, and extending our day a few hours really wouldn't make a great deal of difference. Besides, we know God redeems the time as we are obedient to Him. So, as physically and emotionally drained as we were, we went to the home of Terry Baugh where the home tour was held. What we experienced that afternoon was a total blessing and has thus caused me to write this chapter in *Things Happen When Women Care*.

Here's how "A Different Kind of Christmas" was started.

In July of 1989 a beautiful, blonde homemaker named Terry Baugh began a support group in her home to reach out to her community. God then lifted up another beautiful young mother, Heidi Brown, to support Terry and her vision. Through their Bible study, 2 Corinthians 5:18–6:1 became a challenge to these women: how we as ladies have the responsibility and privilege to be workers together in sharing the message of Jesus with those who do not know Him. Together, Terry and Heidi prayed for their next step. A meeting was called where two other women showed up. They felt the Lord asking them to stand firm on their commitment and what they felt was right. Other women would come in time. They asked the Lord to reveal to them a plan. They were committed to do that plan even if it was just the two of them. It was after that prayer of faith that the Lord revealed "A Different Kind of Christmas."

Here is the step-by-step, detailed walk-through of how Terry and Heidi organized this very beautiful, heart-filled, and heartfelt day (as described by Heidi Brown).

--------------- ♥ ---------------

"A DIFFERENT KIND OF CHRISTMAS"

We began by stepping out in faith and then God gave a picture. We chose a date. We decided December would be a good time because hearts are open and ladies enjoy getting together during the holidays. The year before the Lord had asked me to have a mother/daughter tea for some of my daughter's friends from school. I was able to share the Lord's love with these mothers and that was so exciting. I wanted to do the same thing again, so Terry and I talked about possibly having some kind of a tea or coffee in her home. We proposed in our hearts that we would touch as many women as we possibly could. Then all of a sudden in our discussion the Lord reminded Terry of a home tour held the Christmas of 1988 by our community hospital. Terry and our pastor's wife, Kathy, went through the home tour and enjoyed all the lovely decorations but so desperately felt something was missing. That missing piece was, of course, the Lord...the reason for celebrating Christmas! In our conversation we began to picture a different kind of home tour. The Lord began giving us all the details to this picture. Because my life was impacted and changed at your holiday seminar, Emilie, in December of 1986, I began to share ideas of traditions I had begun in my home over the past three years from your seminar and other sources. The Lord took all of this and gave us this picture of a different kind of Christmas.

We would have a home tour with live narrators throughout the home to explain the true meaning of Christmas and special ideas for traditions and family time. We would not charge any kind of a fee but sell raffle tickets for rag baskets and baked goods for those who would desire to buy them. At the end of the tour we would give each person a gift favor (bean soup) for them to take home and an invitation to come to our church for Christmas services. We also would give them a copy of our women's newsletter with our ideas written out for them to take and try out in their homes. We also felt like a guest book would be good so that if we have another outreach in the future we could invite those ladies who came through the home tour to any future outreaches.

We both got so excited as the Lord was so faithful to help Terry and myself to paint a picture of His plan for our December outreach. Our next step was how could we share our heart of vision so other ladies would join in with us! The Lord reminded us that we "by chance" had just attended a rag-basket-making craft class and we know this too, was not chance. It was something Terry, myself, our pastor's wife had not done in a few years (taking a craft class), but Terry felt drawn to take it and so did I. We decided to draw our ladies in by telling them in a skit at church about our holiday tour and about the rag baskets to be raffled off. We let them know we would teach them how to make one and then asked if they would be willing to donate the first one to our tour. At the time of our skit the Lord had drawn in one of Terry's neighbors who had received Jesus during our Neighborhood Bible Study in Terry's neighborhood. She was so excited about the change the Lord made in her life that she eagerly wanted to share with all her other neighbors through our December outreach. When we did our skit there were four of us committed to our outreach. That next Monday night the Lord drew in the other five ladies that formed our care support group of nine. Later, the Lord added four more committed ladies and then on the day of "A Different Kind of Christmas" we had 26 ladies serving our community with one common purpose: to share Jesus' love and creativity with other women; to be God's ambassadors showing others to the Lord and showing His love for them.

I also wanted to mention that the night Terry and I proposed all this in our hearts with the Lord, we shared it all with Terry's husband, Jim, asking for his opinion and permission to use their home. It was good for us and a challenge to make our appeal to Terry's husband because it made us stronger in our vision. Terry's husband, Jim, is a "caring man" and I truly am grateful to him and my husband, Jim, who is also a very caring man. Their support enabled us in a special way to be caring women. In fact, I know each married woman who took part in this outreach was encouraged by a caring husband. We also had the support of our pastor, Keith, and his wife, Kathy, whose heart is to care, serve, and love others.

The next step in our outreach was the deadlines the Lord gave us for each detail and category needing to be covered. We began in September with specific deadlines to plan for 300 ladies to attend. Here is an example:

- *Due 9/25/89*
  —Sketch of the promo flyer and invitation.
  —List ingredients. Have recipe printed for bean soup favor.
  —Plan our traditions—which ones for which rooms and who will help us. Assign two ladies to each room to narrate traditions.

- *Due 10/9/89*
  —Bean soup favor sample.
  —Decorations planned—what and from whom and when will we pick up.
  —Plan for small children—table/crayons in back-yard with a sitter.

- *Due 10/23/89*
  —Bean soup favors finished—each lady did 30 bags of beans, asking a friend to help her.
  —Rag baskets done—filled with goodies and Scrip-tures and turned in.
  —Music planned.
  —Name tags made for each lady who will be serving.
  —What we will wear—blouse/skirt in red/white/green.

- *Due 11/6/89*
  —Decorations brought in.
  —3 x 5 cards with our traditions written out and copies for newsletter.
  —Raffle details.
  —Guest book.
  —Flyers to pass out (promo).

- *Due 11/13/89*
  —Trial run.
  —Practice walking through.
  —Details ... how many ladies at once—where would they stand, etc.
  —Outside decor—poinsettias—where to purchase.

- *Due 11/27/89 and 12/1/89*
  —Set up and decorate.

- *12/2/89*
  —Day of event.
  —10:00 A.M.—Baked goods ladies to set up and pre-pare food.
  —Come at noon to pray and be prepared.

These detailed deadlines allowed us to be organized and not to feel overwhelmed, rushed, or pressured. We tackled this big job with two-week intervals of smaller jobs.

The Lord faithfully sent a woman who is an artist into our core group. She drew up our invitation and flyer.

The Lord also sent women to help with making and donating baked goods. We have a printer at our church who printed up our flyers and invitations. Ladies donated their finances to buy poinsettias to decorate the outdoors and we then used them to decorate our church sanctuary. He sent us ladies to fill and donate rag baskets. He provided greeters, hostesses, narrators, cashiers, etc. These 26 ladies who came together served that day along with others who helped out as they were needed. They all had the same desire—to reach other women with the life, love, and hope that only our Lord can offer.

------------ ♥ ------------

Over 200 women attended the home tour, along with many men and children. As Bob and I parked that afternoon by Terry and Jim's home, we were greeted by two friendly hostesses. They had hospital-type doctor's booties for us to wear that fit over our shoes. That made us feel comfortable about keeping the floors and carpets clean in Terry's home. We had to wait by the front door until the preceding tour was finished. A lovely hostess began to tell us a little about what we were to experience. She gave us ideas for creating a warm welcome around our own front doors by decorating them with paper-ribbon bells, wreaths, etc.

GRAPEVINE WREATH

Materials Needed: Plain wreath, assorted flowers and ribbon, hot-glue gun. (All are available at craft stores.)

Directions: Carefully cut flowers off of stem (about $1/2$–$1/4''$ down). Glue to wreath, allowing stem to be inserted into spaces between vines on your wreath. Glue on the ribbon. Hot-glue gun is a must. It can be purchased in craft or hardware stores.

We were also able at that time to purchase a ticket for the beautiful rag baskets filled with holiday goodies, mugs, stationery, Scriptures, napkins, teas, nuts, etc. I was excited and hopeful that I could possibly be the recipient of such a lovely care basket. One of the hostesses described how to make a "care basket":

CARE BASKET GIFT IDEA

A "care basket" is a gift basket filled with goodies and paper cut outs (any kind of shape—I use hearts) that have personalized Scriptures written out to the person on them. Begin with a basket, gift bag, tin, plastic colander, bowl or bucket and fill with goodies and Scriptures (examples below). Wrap with colored or clear cellophane and tie with a bow.

FILLING A CARE BASKET

"Personalizing" is the key. Think of the person you are giving the basket to and develop a theme around their likes and dislikes, hobbies, circumstances, needs, etc. Here are a few "theme" ideas:

1) *New neighbors*—kitchen basket, plastic colander filled with kitchen towels, wooden spoons and/or measuring spoons and cups, favorite recipe for muffins or bread (and a sample, of course). Write out the recipe of anything you make. Add some potpourri to simmer on the stove. Include Scriptures encouraging your neighbors in their new move.

2) *A basket idea for a man*—Car-washing sponge/ equipment, soap, etc. A cardboard windshield sun visor, lots of munchies. Wrap in a big plastic bucket.

3) *Christmas basket*—Include a copy of the Christmas card basket tradition (see page 148). Add a pretty kitchen towel, two mugs, some thank-you notes and stamps, muffins and recipe, and a Christmas music tape. Encourage your friends to use their basket this year and try the Christmas card tradition, sending some thank-yous to those who sent cards or gave gifts (good idea for a teacher).

Soon over 20 people had gathered and we were ushered into the home. It was like a fairyland of holiday warmth. The living room hostess greeted us and began to give ideas and the meaning of the tree, lights, and manger. Another hostess read the Christmas story from Luke 2.

Not only did she suggest having a family tree ornament party, but she gave us all the following recipe:

HOMEMADE CHRISTMAS ORNAMENTS

Set aside an evening for making homemade Christmas ornaments, drinking hot chocolate, singing Christmas carols, and enjoying your family. You can string popcorn and cranberries to make garlands. It's fun and easy to do! Or try some cutout clay cookies using the following recipe:

Ingredients:

$1\frac{1}{2}$ c. flour
$\frac{1}{2}$ c. salt
$\frac{1}{4}$ c. oil
$\frac{1}{2}$ c. water

Mix flour and salt in bowl. Slowly stir in water and oil. Squeeze mixture for about 3-4 minutes until it feels like clay.

Roll out to about ⅛" thickness, and cut out with Christmas cookie cutters. Pierce small hole to use for hanging with ornament hook. They will air-dry in 2–3 days. Paint with tempera paints. Spray with aerosol glaze (called "clear glaze"—you can find it in any craft store). Glue on ribbon, etc. for additional decorations.

Here are some interesting and creative ideas the living room hostess shared with us for the nativity.

NATIVITY SCENE

- Leave your Bible open to Luke, chapter two, in front of the nativity scene to remind everyone of its meaning. Make time to read aloud the Scripture passage with family and friends.

- To count down the days till Christmas, use the "baby Jesus" and daily move Him closer to His manger until Christmas Eve. Have one family member designated to place Him in His manger.

- As Jesus is making His way to the manger have another tradition where the children add one piece of straw to Jesus' bed for every good deed that they do . . . softening the bed of our Lord!

FAMILY TIME AROUND THE TREE

- Devote one evening to a person you know is spending the holidays alone. Make sure to plan the evening to make that person feel a part of your family, not just a spectator.

- Devote an evening to sitting around your tree sharing special memories of favorite Christmases of the past. Be sure to allow each person to have a turn.

- Cut down a Christmas tree as a family—it's a great tradition to start. Spend the day together selecting your tree and cutting it down, and have a special tree-decorating party. Add a traditional snack or full-meal menu. Sing or listen to Christmas carols as you decorate.

- Another tradition around the tree could be during the Christmas morning gift opening. Designate one person to pass out the gifts. Allow the "helper" to change year to year. Why not try youngest to oldest? Also, try opening your gifts one at a time so that everyone may share and experience the "joy of giving and receiving" of each gift.

This living room presentation took all of 4–7 minutes.

From there we focused on the dining room where the table was beautifully set and two other hostesses welcomed us.

Here is what they shared as we listened eagerly.

———————— ♥ ————————

WELCOME TO CHRISTMAS IN OUR DINING ROOM

The dining room is a cherished place in our home throughout the year. It is a place where we can all come together as a family and share together intimately in conversation. This is not too difficult in our home right now because our children are small and at home. I realize that as they grow and begin to develop their own outside activities, it will be more difficult to keep our special mealtimes together. I know one creative mom who, along with her family, decided to have their largest meal of the day in the morning because that was the only time all their schedules would be in harmony, thus keeping their special time together around their table possible.

During the Christmas holidays in our home, our dining room table remains that place where intimate time is shared with close friends and family. I enjoy setting a table that is not only pretty and festive but more importantly says to the person, "Welcome," "Come sit down," and "You are special." To begin with, here are a few special touches you can add to your dining room table:

1. *Candles.* Candles add warmth to our table. They say "Welcome." The traditional meaning of candles was to express goodwill and affection. Candles signify the light that Jesus shed on our world when He was born. I use candles in my main centerpiece and also as a special take-home favor. A set of small string candles are tied with Christmas ribbon and a special greeting. My greeting says this: "These candles symbolize the 'true' light, warmth, and love that was shed on our world during the first Christmas. May you experience this same light, love, and warmth during this holiday season and carry it with you throughout the year."

2. *Name cards.* Personal name cards express to your guests that they were specifically planned for. Inside each name card I write that person's name and its meaning (which can be found in a name book). As we begin our conversation time, I ask each person to go around the room and read the meaning of their name and use that to impart to us something about themselves. This is an excellent way to "break the ice" in conversation and learn a little bit more about each other.

3. *Napkin rings.* They add personality to your table. Usually the napkin rings on my table express a little bit about me or a special meaning I'd like to share with my guests. For example, you might want to use a candy-cane-wreath napkin ring. These are colorful and the wreath is an expression of love and faith. The circular shape is a symbol of God's never-ending love for us.

These are small extra touches that take extra time and effort, but the expression of love in them is well-expressed and well-received. It is worth the extra time and work. The following are special traditions done at our dining room table with our family:

4. *Hat centerpiece.* This hat was decorated with lace and silk flowers by a friend for me last Christmas. Around the edges of the hat she glued 31 ribbons to hold 31 scrolls of paper rolled up. Each night at the end of our mealtime we unwrap one of our scrolls of paper and read it out loud (my husband usually does this). Written on the scroll is a special word of blessing, a Scripture for our family, or a Scripture that describes the very first Christmas. After we read it we discuss it as a family and then close with a short time of prayer to seal this into our hearts. It is a special time together to focus on the "true" meaning of Christmas—the Lord Jesus.

5. *Advent calendar.* Another tradition similar to this is an Advent calendar with a Scripture to read, discuss, and pray about together. This calendar has been a wonderful tool with our children. We burn a candle down for five minutes each night as we share about the Scripture for that particular day and then blow the candle out when we are finished. We use it again the next night going through the same process until we've gone through the whole calendar.

6. *Sending Christmas cards . . . something to think about.* Is this a tradition in your home, or are you wondering if you want to begin this tradition? Why not ask yourself why you send Christmas cards:

- To express Christmas wishes?

- To tell the gospel message of Christ's birth?

- To enjoy a special Christmas tradition that is meaningful?

- To fulfill others' expectations?

- To thank special people in your life?

- To affirm and strengthen relationships?

7. *Christmas card basket.* This special decorated basket is placed near our table. Each day as we receive our Christmas cards in the mail, we place them inside the basket. We take turns picking a card each night and pray for the sender of that card. Sometimes I will write the sender a special note letting them know we covered them in prayer. This tradition can continue on into the first of the year.

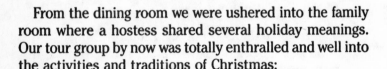

From the dining room we were ushered into the family room where a hostess shared several holiday meanings. Our tour group by now was totally enthralled and well into the activities and traditions of Christmas:

WELCOME TO CHRISTMAS IN OUR FAMILY ROOM

Story of St. Nicholas. Remember that Santa is *not* God in a red suit. St. Nicholas was a very generous man that lived in the fourth century in Turkey. He earned the reputation of a man of compassion and conscience and he was a church leader who was willing to stand up against the injustices of his time. After his death in A.D. 343, stories grew out of proportion into what is now Santa, miracle, and magic.

Gift-giving. Teach your children to be givers of gifts who demonstrate love and generosity and devotion. They can help spread the glad anticipation and generous spirit that Santa represents. A beautiful way to remember the true spirit of Christmas morning is to mark a wrapped box with "Open Me First" addressed to the family. Inside place a note saying, "This box is filled with enough peace and love to last all year. Share it generously and you'll find a renewed Christmas spirit this day." Gift ideas: picnic basket filled with deli items; toolbox, partly equipped; set of mugs with a pound of coffee beans; box of stationery and stamps; a recipe with essential ingredients; basket filled with home-made bread, etc.

Stockings. Long before Christmas trees became a tradi-tion, stockings were hung along the fireplace in anticipa-tion of Santa's visit. Today's stockings are far different. Instead of everyday stockings, we make them oversized and specially decorated. Fill stockings with only written or symbolic gifts. Hang a stocking for baby Jesus and let each family member make a written promise: a check for world hunger, a symbol of an intention to change a bad habit, etc.

The Yule log. This log was chosen carefully, trimmed, and dragged home. Once inside, it was rolled to the fire-place to burn through Christmas. In Christian tradition the log was from an ash tree because the infant Jesus was first washed and dressed alongside an ash fire. Gather the fam-ily around the fire, each with their own project (reading, knitting, etc.), listen to carols, and enjoy a light snack.

Bells. Christians used bells to call believers to worship. Bells were also used as protectors to tell of storms and terrify evil spirits. An hour before midnight on Christmas Eve many countries rang bells to warn Satan of Christ's birth. At midnight they'd sound triumphantly of Satan's death and the Savior's birth. Use bells in many of your Christmas decorations or gifts.

Christmas caroling. This tradition did not start until 1660 in England. Many of the carols we know today were written in the 1800's. Gather family and friends for caroling, making a "star" to carry with you. Strike up a holiday band—start recruiting in summer.

Poinsettias. The poinsettia is called the "flame leaf" because its leaves turn brilliant red around Christmastime. The plant is also called the "flower of the holy night." It adds beautiful Christmas color.

Holly. According to legend, the crown of thorns was wound with holly and the white berries turned red after the crucifixion. In France and England, this prickly plant was hung over doors to show that Christ resided therein. Decorate home and gifts with holly sprigs.

Holiday baking. Baking can show the love and generosity in our hearts as we give gifts of baked goods to family and friends. Traditional breads (cranberry, gingerbread) are among the favorites. Cookies are fun to decorate with your children, and making a gingerbread house is fun for all.

———— ♥ ————

Here's a story and recipe one hostess shared with us that she tells as her grandchildren bake cookies:

———— ♥ ————

CHRIST-CENTERED COOKIE CUTTER CREATIONS

Prepare yourself for a special time with your family by spending time in the kitchen baking Christmas cookies. Forget the mess that is about to be made. Flour dough, sprinkles, and frosting can always be cleaned up. The important part is what will be taught and fed to the hearts of your family during the next hour.

- *Cookie Cutter #1—Christmas Tree.* What's this? It's a Christmas tree. Do you like Christmas? I love

Christmas. What goes under the Christmas tree? Presents. Do you like presents? I love presents. I wonder who gave the first present or who received the first present? I don't know.

- *Cookie Cutter #2—Angel.* There were three very wise men. An angel came to them and told them to look up in the sky and they saw a star.

- *Cookie Cutter #3—Star.* The angel told the three wise men to follow the star and, when they did, it took them to Bethlehem where they found our Lord. They gave Him their gifts: a bag of gold, a jar of frankincense, the perfume of flowers sort of like potpourri, and a special box of myrrh—the perfume of spices.

- *Cookie Cutter #4—Heart.* The heart represents love. What do you think of when you see the heart? Love, right? Do you know that God loves you and He loved you so much He gave you a sacrificial gift, His Son, Jesus Christ? Sacrificial? What's that? Well... do you have something that you really love—more than almost anything? You only have one like it— maybe a special blanket—and you give it away. Well, that's what sacrificial means. Let's say all you had in the whole world was one dollar and you were hungry but you saw someone else who was also hungry. You took your dollar and bought the other hungry person food. That would be giving a sacrifice.

- *Cookie Cutter #5—Cross.* The cross represents life. The cross represents Jesus, the reason for the season. The baby Jesus grew up and He learned to walk and talk and became a man. He went to the cross and died for our sins—past, present, and future. When we believe in Him, He forgives us our sins and gives us eternal life. It never ends; it goes on forever and ever, eternally. When Jesus died, He went to heaven to be with His heavenly Father; however, He left the Holy Spirit with us.

- *Cookie Cutter #6—Dove.* The dove represents God's Spirit. The Spirit of Jesus lives within us when we believe and receive Him into our life, which means we are never alone. God is always with us, to love and comfort us.

- *Cookie Cutter #7—Church.* The church represents worship. Do you like church? What do you do in church? We sing, listen to or read Bible stories, pray, and worship God. Yes, church is a very special time in our week. It's also a place where we can bring friends to hear about the Lord and to fellowship with each other.

- *Cookie Cutter #8—Candle.* The candle represents light. Matthew 5:16 says we are to let our light shine. Our faith, thoughts, and feelings are to be full of light. Light gives a welcome feeling. Christmas gives us a special opportunity to let our light shine. We can tell others about Jesus and that Christmas is His birthday.

We then bake our cookies and decorate them. I pour juice or milk, and we overdose on cookies. No way can we eat them all! Into the freezer the rest go. A few days before Christmas, out come the cookies. We put them in baggies or on a paper plate covered with clear wrap and a bow. The children put one package in their wagon, doll stroller, or in a big basket and take Christ-centered cookies, one of each shape, and deliver them to all the neighbors. The neighbors may not know the meaning of each of the cookie shapes, but those who made them do. We've not only taught the children to bake cookies, but we've taught them much more. They know the story of Christmas and the message of Jesus. They have also learned to give a sacrificial gift of cookies to those who may not have any Christ-centered cookies.

You can adapt your own story to each of the eight shapes if you like. This is just an idea and a place to start. Additional cutters can be purchased in gourmet shops or kitchen specialty stores.

The hostess then shared the following recipe with us:

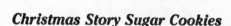

Christmas Story Sugar Cookies

This recipe is suited to cookie cutters. Tell your children all the different aspects of the Christmas story and traditions as you bake these together, creating stars, hearts, trees, angels, and animals. Practically any cookie-cutter shape can suggest a biblical truth that you can teach the children as you enjoy baking together for the holidays.

Makes 3–4 dozen cookies.

1. Preheat oven to 375° F. Blend dry ingredients and set aside:

    2½ cups whole wheat pastry flour (available at health food stores)

    1 Tbsp. cinnamon, optional

    ½ tsp. nutmeg, optional

    1 tsp. baking powder

    1 tsp. salt

2. Whip butter until creamy; blend in fructose and vanilla; blend in eggs:

    ½ cup butter

    ⅔ cup crystalline fructose (available at health food stores)

    1 tsp. vanilla extract

    2 eggs

3. Blend the dry ingredients into the liquid ingredients until nicely blended, but do not overbeat as this will toughen the dough.

4. Divide dough in half and chill several hours or overnight.

5. Remove half the dough from refrigerator at a time. Press flat with palm of hand on evenly floured surface. A Tupperware pastry sheet is ideal.

6. Lay a piece of wax paper over top of dough and roll out with a rolling pin to about ⅛" thick. Peel wax paper off and replace occasionally while rolling out.

7. Dip cookie cutters in flour and cut. Gently press scraps together and roll out lightly as needed to cut remaining dough.

8. Place cookies on ungreased cookie sheets. Interesting designs may be made in cookies with a toothpick and the end of a straw.

9. Bake at 375° for 6 to 8 minutes; remove to wire cake rack to cool. Decorate as desired before or after baking.[1]

———— ♥ ————

The following is another wonderful story the hostess shared with us:

———— ♥ ————

SANTA CLAUS

Many people do not know that there is a special story about who Santa Claus really is. There was a special Christian man who lived a long time ago. His name was Nicholas, and we call him St. Nicholas because saint means someone who belongs to God. In St. Nicholas' town there were many poor children. They didn't have enough food, clothes, or toys. St. Nicholas used his money to buy food, clothes, and toys for the poor children. He didn't want them to be embarrassed by his gifts, so he gave them secretly.

St. Nicholas also told everyone about Jesus and how much God loved them. Many people became Christians because of what St. Nicholas said. Then some mean people who hated Jesus put St. Nicholas in jail to keep him from telling people about Jesus and from helping people. St. Nicholas continued to tell people about Jesus until the mean people finally had him killed.

Because of how much St. Nicholas loved Jesus, and because of the many gifts he gave the poor children in his town, we still remember St. Nicholas at Christmastime. All of the gifts he gave and all of the gifts we give are to remind us of the very best gift anyone ever gave . . . when God the Father gave His only Son, Jesus Christ, to us for our salvation.

—Gretchen Passantino
Discipleship Journal

———— ♥ ————

Bob and I began to feel the blessings offered to us by these women during the home tour. A reverence began to exude from our group. You could hear a pin drop. Next we went into the kitchen where the smells and aromas flowed. Samples of yummy foods were displayed and two other hostesses shared.

———— ♥ ————

Wassail Bowl

This hot cider, fruit, and spice drink began in England. It was customary for every family to have a wassail bowl steaming away through the Christmas season. It was served to carolers that visited the house. Here is Emilie's wassail bowl recipe:

> In a large pot or Crockpot combine:
> 1 gallon apple cider
> 1 large can pineapple juice
> 1 cup strong tea or herb tea

> In a cloth sack, put:
> 1 Tbsp. whole cloves
> 1 Tbsp. whole all-spice
> 2 cinnamon sticks

> Tie with a string or thread and put into wassail mix. Simmer for 4–8 hours. Water can be added if the wassail gets too strong toward the bottom.

Next our hostess shared the following with us:

———————— ♥ ————————

Happy Birthday, Jesus

Sometimes we forget that Christmas is a month-long birthday for Jesus. The guest of honor may be unseen, but His presence is assured. Have a party; bake a cake. Make a "Happy Birthday Jesus," banner with your children. Read the Christmas story (Luke 2:4-20) and have each party guest act out a part.

Christmas Breakfast

Our memories are full of joy, laughter, and heartfelt moments as we begin this very special day. Set a beautiful table and, as you light candles, sing a Christmas carol as a thanksgiving grace. Then partake of some yummy treats: Fruit Soup and Almond Crunch Coffee Cake. Here are the recipes for our holiday breakfast favorites (also great for company year-round):

Fruit Soup

8–10 servings

(Our hostess said that her friend Carole gave her this recipe, and she uses it winter and summer. It's fresh and delicious and always gets compliments.)

Stir 3 tablespoons of quick-cooking tapioca into 1 cup water in a small saucepan; add a pinch of salt. Heat to a full, rolling boil, stirring constantly. Pour into a medium-sized bowl. Stir in one 6-oz. can of frozen orange juice (concentrate) until melted. Add 1½ cups of water. Cool 15 minutes then add 2 cups of fresh or canned peaches, 1 fresh orange, 1 banana, 1 cup seedless green grapes and 1 tablespoon lemon juice. Chill covered. It will thicken in a few hours. Serve in fruit cups or in pretty stem glasses.

Almond Crunch Coffee Cake

Preheat oven to 350°.
Grease a 9″ x 13″ cake pan.
For topping, blend together until crumbly:
   ¼ cup whole wheat pastry flour
   2 Tbsp. granulated fructose
   1 Tbsp. soft butter

Stir into topping mixture and set aside:
   ½ cup chopped almonds

Blend together thoroughly:
   2 eggs
   ¾ cup honey

Mix in:
  1 cup buttermilk

Blend dry ingredients together:

  2 cups whole wheat pastry flour
  2 tsp. cinnamon
  1 tsp. baking powder
  1 tsp. soda
  ½ tsp. salt
  ¼ tsp. ginger

Blend dry ingredients into liquid ingredients until smooth.

Pour batter into greased pan and top evenly with almond topping. Press topping slightly into batter with tines of a fork.

Bake about 30 minutes until knife inserted in center comes out clean.[2]

Huevos Rancheros

2 Servings

A hearty dish suitable for breakfast as well as lunch or dinner.

Blend together in small fry pan:
  1 cup natural pasta sauce or tomato sauce
  1 Tbsp. or more diced green chiles, to taste
  ⅜ tsp. cumin powder, to taste

Heat just until sauce is bubbling. Lower heat and break into sauce:
  2 eggs

Cover and cook until eggs are set to desired doneness.

Over gas burner or in oven heat until crisp:

2 stoneground corn tortillas (tortillas may be crisped in hot oil and drained on paper towel, but I try to avoid the extra fat).

Set tortillas on individual plates.

Slide 1 egg with sauce onto each corn tortilla.

Top each with:
¼ cup grated cheddar or jack cheese
chopped chives or green onion

Cheesy Egg Muffin

1 Serving

Toast and butter lightly:
1 whole-grain English muffin half

Top with:
1 scrambled egg
2 Tbsp. grated cheddar or jack cheese

Warm in oven, under broiler, or in toaster oven until cheese melts.

Variations: for added flavor, add diced chiles, chopped green onion, mushrooms, or whatever you desire, to scrambled egg.[3]

Hot Cocoa Mix Recipe

Package in jars with pretty Christmas bow or lace.

Ingredients:
1 - 8-qt. box powdered milk
1 - 6-oz. jar Cremora
1 - 1-lb. box Nestlés Quik
2 tsp. cinnamon

Mix all ingredients together in large bowl. Add 3 heaping tablespoons of Hot Cocoa Mix to mug full of hot water and stir.

———————— ♥ ————————

As our tour group left the kitchen with its warm, fragrant atmosphere, we were given recipes and samples. I didn't want this special time to end. This small church in the Santa Clarita Valley of California (Desert Streams Church of the Open Door) truly gave us all the touch of "A Different Kind of Christmas"—Christmas with heart and meaning. God does give us all special abilities and opportunities to minister and influence lives for His kingdom. This women's ministry cared for the hearts of their community. Their prayer is that this occasion will be repeated in churches throughout the nation and others will feel "the reason for the season" and be touched with a different kind of Christmas—not as the world gives, but as Christ meant for it to be. As Christians, it's Christmas in our hearts all year long, and December is a special month to expand on the wonderful gift God has given us through His Son, Jesus, who has come to bring life—eternal life! May we continually desire to exalt His name and declare His wonderful works to people around us.

Our tour was almost over. Leaving the kitchen, we went to the courtyard where tables were set with cakes and cookies and yummy homemade foods to purchase. As we left, a hostess gave us a gift bag of bean soup and an outline of what we had just experienced (along with a warm invitation of welcome to their church).

We were so refreshed and blessed. I couldn't wait to go home and create "A Different Kind of Christmas" of our own.

At my annual Christmas tea for my close friends, I shared with them that day in Santa Clarita, California. I told them the meanings of the holly, bells, Yule log, poinsettias, and

St. Nicholas. Our time ended with sharing and tears. It was a wonderful day filled with "A Different Kind of Christmas."

Thank you, Desert Streams Church, for allowing the Spirit of God to touch your community and our lives—all because you *cared*.

I've concluded this chapter with a poem that came across my desk. I don't know who wrote it, but it says it all.

———————— ♥ ————————

'TWAS THE NIGHT BEFORE JESUS CAME

'Twas the night before Jesus came and all through the house
Not a creature was praying, not one in the house.
Their Bibles were lain on the shelf without care
In hopes that Jesus would not come there.

The children were dressing to crawl into bed,
Not once ever kneeling or bowing a head.
And Mom in her rocker with baby on her lap
Was watching the Late Show while I took a nap.

When out of the East there arose such a clatter,
I sprang to my feet to see what was the matter.
Away to the window I flew like a flash
Tore open the shutters and threw up the sash!

When what to my wondering eyes should appear
But angels proclaiming that Jesus was here.
With a light like the sun sending forth a bright ray
I knew in a moment this must be THE DAY!

The light of His face made me cover my head.
It was Jesus! Returning just like He had said.
And though I possessed worldly wisdom and wealth,
I cried when I saw Him in spite of myself.

In the Book of Life which He held in His hand,
Was written the name of every saved man.
He spoke not a word as He searched for my name;
When He said "It's not here," my head hung in shame.

The people whose names had been written with love
He gathered to take to His Father above.
With those who were ready He rose without a sound
While all the rest were left standing around.

I fell to my knees, but it was too late;
I had waited too long and thus sealed my fate.
I stood and I cried as they rose out of sight;
Oh, if only I had been ready tonight.

In the words of this poem the meaning is clear;
The coming of Jesus is drawing near.
There's only one life and when comes the last call
We'll find that the Bible was true after all!

—Author Unknown

————— ♥ —————

*Love is what you've
lived through with someone.*

8 | *Caring Through Meeting the Needs of the Heart*

—————— ♥ ——————

> *[A woman] well-known for her good deeds, such as bringing up children, showing hospitality, washing the feet of the saints, helping those in trouble* (1 Timothy 5:10 NIV).

*S*EVERAL YEARS AGO Sue Gregg, the coauthor of *Eating Right*, published by Harvest House, and I attended the same small community church in Riverside. Being small in size let us know at a very intimate level the needs of the families in our fellowship. We knew when there were tears of joy and tears of pain; we knew of weddings, births, separations, divorce, and death. Being such a close-knit group, there was always need for prayer, comfort, encouragement, carpooling, running errands, and food preparation. Since organization is my expertise and balanced cooking and healthy foods is Sue's joy, we raised our hands to bring together a combined effort to organize the *care* ministry of our church.

We set out to establish a "labor of love" for our families. Since then, Sue and I have had the opportunity to share not only the concepts but the plans and various forms we used in administering this very successful ministry.

There are many people who want to help others in their needs, but don't really know how or what to do and say. Maybe our experience can be of help to you as you care for others.

As we began to look at our new ministry, we decided to work through the acrostic C-A-R-E.

C   **Creative Purpose**
- Who We Care For
- Why We Care
- How We Care

A   **Active Preparation**
- The Plan
- Working the Plan

R   **Realistic Presentation**
- Demonstration of Foods
- The Plan Works for You

E   **Entertaining Pleasure**
- Preparing the Place
- What to Say
- Crisis Checklist

As we thought through the purposes for this ministry, we wanted to define those areas of care we were to minister to. We didn't want to take too big of an area of responsibility or our resources would be reduced to an ineffective mess. We arrived at short-term cares that needed a visitation, a card of encouragement, a telephone call to see if there were any needs that we could meet, a meal, a prayer, etc. See Exhibit E on page 166 that shows the chart we used in gathering information on a person's needs. Once we knew the scope of our ministry, we were able to train various other helping families to carry out their all-important ministry. We had workshops at our kitchens to show how helpers could prepare healthy, nutritious foods and also meet the unique nutritional needs of each family.

We soon developed a CARE notebook which gave all the necessary answers that one would need to assist in this ministry. Our notebook contained information on:

- CARE-Request information forms
- What You Can Say
- A Crisis Checklist
- Calendars—Yearly
     —Daily Schedule
     —Month-on-a-Page
- Important Telephone Numbers
- Items Loaned/Borrowed
- Expenses
- Prayer Requests
- Sources and Resources
- Menus/Recipes
- Shopping List
- Weekly Menus
- Notes

If you become challenged in this area of *care* for the families of your church, social group, or neighborhood, you may order these forms from our ministry. See page 6 for our mailing address.

Sue and I soon realized the need for one form that would list all needs and would give all the necessary information to committee members. This is where I really got excited about making a useful all-purpose form. See Exhibit E on page 166. This form was printed on regular 20# stock. When a need in our church was identified, we would fill out all the necessary information. Depending upon the specific needs of the party, we would delegate the responsibility to various members of our committee. We worked very closely with the pastors and the board of elders. Many times they would let us know of specific needs and there were times we would let them know of hurts in the body of believers. Our services were open not only to members of our church, but to friends, relatives, or neighbors of those in the church. Because of time and travel constraints,

CARE – REQUEST INFORMATION FORM

Person requesting assistance __Mary Ann Glee__ Address __2447 "E" St.__ Phone __622-4714__

Name of person in need __Joe & Ann Nobley__ Address __11177 Ash__ Phone __683-2607__

Age __54__ Situation: Illness: ☒ At home ☐ Hospital ☐ Other _____ Phone __683-2607__

Date __7/1/90__ Death: Funeral Home _____ Address _____ Room # ____ Phone ____

☐ Out of state: Where: ____ Address ____ Phone ____

Family/friend of: ____

Crisis: ☐ Separation ☐ Divorce ☐ Job ☐ Other ____

Birth: ☐ Hospital ____ Address ____ Room # ____ Phone ____

Other: ____

Care need: ☒ Visitation ☒ Phone call ☒ Prayer ☒ Meals ☐ Other ____

Dates needed __7/1/90 – 7/4/90__ Quantity needed __4 in family__

HEALTH PROBLEM(S)	DIET RECOMMENDATION: ☐ DOCTOR'S ORDERS ☐ PERSONAL CHOICE	GENERAL GUIDELINES FOR MEALS AND/OR RECIPES USED	MEALS NEEDED		
			Date	Menu/Recipes	Provided by
☐ Heart Attack	☐ No Salt	☐ Provide Dinners on Weekdays	7/1	#1	Jones'
☐ Surgery	☐ Low Salt	☐ Provide Sunday PM Break	7/2	#2	Levin's
☐ Diabetes	☐ Low Fat	☐ Use Saltless Recipes	7/3	#3	DeLorenzo's
☐ Birth	☐ Low Cholesterol	☐ No Eggs in Recipes	7/4	#4	Merrihew's
☐ Kidney Disease	☐ No Fresh Vegetables	☐ All Vegetables Cooked			
☐ Stroke	☐ Low Calorie	☐ No Beef		SERVE BETWEEN	
☐ High Blood Pressure	☐ Low Meat	☐ No Meat of any kind		5:30–6:00pm	
☐ Allergies	☒ No Meat	Special Likes:			
☐ Overweight	☒ Chicken/Fish Only	1. general			
☐ Cerebral Palsy	☐ Allergies:	2.			
☐ Senility	1. none	3.			
☐ Osteoporosis	2.	Dislikes:			
☒ Other __Auto__	3.	1. none			
__accident__	☐ No Refined Sugar	2.			
	☐ No Refined Flour	3.			
	☐ Other ____	☐ Other ____			

people usually did need to live geographically close to our church. However, on many occasions we would send a card, make a telephone call, or write a letter of encouragement to those out of our area. We received back notes and letters of appreciation for our thoughtfulness and concern. The body of Christ cares.

As you can readily see by looking at this form, we can provide our committee members with all the basic information we would need in order to help out our person(s) in need. The top half of the form gives basic data and the bottom half gives information for consideration in preparing proper food for the person(s).

Sue and I found that many well-meaning ladies of our committee had no training in cooking proper foods for people with specific dietary needs. This gave us a great opportunity to be a Titus 2:3-5 woman, which states that older women are to be teachers to the younger women. We found the women to be very excited learners and doers. The basis of our teaching was found in Sue's and my book *Eating Right—A Realistic Approach to a Healthy Lifestyle*, published by Harvest House. We supplemented this book with eight other cookbooks that Sue and I have self-published through Eating Better Publications:

The Busy Woman's Main Dish Book

The Busy Woman's Breakfast Book

The Busy Woman's Muffin/Soup Book

The Busy Woman's Lunch and Snack Book

The Busy Woman's Casserole Book

The Busy Woman's Dessert Book

The Busy Woman's Yeast Bread Book

The Holiday Menu Planner

This package of books gave us all the food data someone would need to provide healthy and nutritious foods to those in need. We wanted to get away from high fats, sugar, high salts, and low-fiber meals. And we certainly wanted to get beyond the fast-food mindset. Sue and I were amazed to see how the ladies in the committee began to change their own style of cooking for their families once they realized how they were literally poisoning their loved ones (not intentionally) by the food they prepared and served. (Why do we have to wait for our loved ones to have high blood pressure, high cholesterol, a stroke, a heart attack, or colon cancer before we listen to wise advice from our doctors?)

This form also gave us a record of when meals were needed and who was going to provide the meals. We would follow up on the day of the need to the person preparing the meal, stating just a reminder of the particulars. The follow-up is very important because we live in a very busy world with people who are tangled up in busyness. A brief reminder saves potential embarrassments.

What You Can Say

Many of us are well-meaning in time of need, but aren't always sure of what to say and how to say it. We wanted our committee to go through some training in this area. We selected, from a new book by a very close friend of ours, Lauren Littauer Briggs (*What You Can Say... When You Don't Know What to Say*—Harvest House Publishers), some helpful statements of do's and don'ts when we are comforting those in need. Lauren's helpful advice was:

"WHAT YOU CAN SAY..."

The following suggestions are not word-for-word statements to make, but rather a reflection of a heart attitude you should have in reaching out to your hurting person. May God fill you with His tenderness and compassion, enabling you to be an extension of His love.

Helpful Statements for Comforting Those in Need

	Do Say	Don't Say
At a funeral	I'll always remember . . . I'll come by with dinner tonight.	He's so much better off in heaven. If there's anything I can do, call.
A baby died	I know how much being a mother means to you.	You can always have another one. Be thankful you have Jenny. At least you never got to know it.
Divorce	The future must seem frightening. I'll stay close. I'm sure this is a lonely time for you— Let's have lunch.	I never liked the way he treated you. There are two sides to every story.
Legal crisis	It's not important what happened. I just want you to know that I care.	Will you lose everything? Tell me how it happened.
Handicapped child	She has beautiful eyes. She is so loving and precious.	What are you going to do with her? If you'd taken better care of yourself this wouldn't have happened.
Elderly parent	I know how much you love her. I'm sure you're doing the right thing.	How could you put your own mother in such a place?

(Continued)

	Do Say	*Don't Say*
Loss of home	I've been a part of some very beautiful memories here.	Remember, our home is really in heaven.
Friend moving	I've seen what special friends you are. I know you'll miss each other.	Well, you can always write.
Pet dies	I know she was important to your family. Sometimes this brings back other sad feelings.	It's only a dog! You can always buy a new kitten.
During terminal illness	How do you feel about what you're facing? I'll take you to your next doctor's appointment.	I know a lady who had the same thing . . . Won't you be glad to be with the Lord?
After death of terminally ill	Even though he needed a lot of your time, I know you'll miss his company.	It must be such a relief now that it's over.
Death of a spouse	I know how much he meant to you, and how you'll miss him.	You were so lucky to have him for 30 years.
Loss of a body	I'm sure this will take a lot of adjustment. I'll be with you every step of the way	At least you still have your mind. Be glad it wasn't worse.[1]

HELPFUL STATEMENTS FOR COMFORTING THOSE IN NEED (Continued)

Time spent in reviewing this area really provided key information for our committee. It certainly helped keep us from saying well-meaning but wrong words. We wanted healing and caring words to be spoken over the phone or in a card or letter. The person in need must really feel that you care and want to be of help. The comments under "don't" make you a judge and evaluator rather than an observer who wants to meet the person in need where he or she is.

A Crisis Checklist

Lauren was also able to assist us by giving from her book several pointers to consider when a crisis appears. These became most informative and certainly provided good information in handling the emergencies when they arose. Crises usually happen at inopportune times—times when we are busy, involved in our own lives and its requirements. So when a crisis catches us off guard, we need to automatically have a basis for responding to the needs of the moment.

For the first time in many of our lives, we realized that there was a proper way to respond to a crisis situation. We wanted to come to our people with open and loving arms. Many times they did not know us very well, and those first few hours and days made a big impact on how they responded to our help.

------------ ♥ ------------

A CRISIS CHECKLIST

DO

Respond in a timely manner with a card, a call, or a visit.

DON'T

Don't wait a long time before you make your initial contact.

DO

Offer simple, understanding statements such as: "I feel for you during this difficult time." "This must be very hard for you." "I share your feelings of loss." "I wish I could take the hurt away." Comments like these let the person know you acknowledge their pain and it's okay for them to feel that way.

DON'T

Don't try to minimize their pain with comments like, "It's probably for the best." "Things could be worse." "You'll remarry." "You're young—you can always have another one." "You're strong, you'll get over it soon." "You know God is in control." Comments like these might be an attempt to offer hope, but to a hurting person, they sound as though you don't comprehend the enormity of what's happened.

DO

Say "I'm so sorry." Then add, "I know how special he was to you." "I'll miss her also." "I want to help you; I'm available anytime you need me." "I've been praying for you. Is there something specific I should be praying for?"

DON'T

Don't say "I'm so sorry," and end the sentence. Your hurting friend is probably sorry, too, but he can't respond to that kind of comment.

DO

Be aggressive with your willingness to help. Ask yourself, "What would I need if I were in a similar situation?" Offer specific things you can do for them like, "I'm on my way to the store. What can I pick up for you?" "Would tomorrow be a good day to help you with the laundry?" "Would the children like to come over and play this afternoon?" Most of the time, a person in crisis can't decide what he does need. Besides, he probably doesn't want to impose.

DON'T

Don't just say, "Is there anything I can do to help?"

DO

Encourage them to keep a journal or write down their thoughts and feelings. Often, just seeing their thoughts on paper helps them deal with what they are facing.

DON'T

Don't say, "You shouldn't feel that way."

DO

Agree when the individual expresses their feelings. Say, "Yes, what happened to you isn't fair and doesn't make any sense," whether or not you share the same perspective.

DON'T

Don't offer spiritual answers as to why they're facing this problem or tell them that they'll be a stronger person afterward. We don't know why tragedies happen—or why certain people have to go through such trauma. We do our friends a disservice by offering possible explanations.

DO

Allow them all the time they need to deal effectively with all the phases of their grief.

DON'T

Don't put timetables on your hurting friend's recovery. Your inference that they're not coping well or should be their old self by now only hinders their progress.

DO

Give spiritual encouragement from your heart, and include Bible verses that have comforted you at a difficult time.

DON'T

Don't quote Bible verses as a way to correct or minimize their feelings. Think very carefully, asking yourself if a passage will communicate comfort or condemnation. Never offer spiritual suggestions from a position of superiority or self-righteousness.

DO

Carefully consider what you can and would like to do. Be creative. Use your gifts and talents to help. Your willing spirit and creative efforts will minister to your hurting friend.

DON'T

Don't put yourself under pressure to perform tasks that you really don't want to do.

DO

Be honest about your experiences. If you haven't endured their particular kind of tragedy say, "I haven't been through what you're facing, but I want you to know I care about you and will support you through the difficult time ahead." If you've had a similar crisis, tell them about it briefly, adding that you can empathize with their feelings. Of course, you can't completely understand because you haven't been through the past experiences that laid the foundation for their reaction.

DON'T

Don't say "I understand" when you haven't faced the same situation. Telling someone that everything will be all right when you have never known the depth of their hardship is an empty statement. And they don't need to hear horror stories of people you know who have been through something similar.

DO

Continue keeping in touch, letting them know you're praying for them. Ask how they're really doing and send thoughtful notes with encouraging words.

DON'T

Don't ignore their needs after the immediate crisis has subsided.

DO

Respond cautiously and prayerfully with uplifting and edifying ideas when friends ask for your help in their tragedy.

DON'T

Don't offer unasked-for advice. If they weren't solicited, your suggestions may not be appreciated.

DO

Provide long-term, unconditional support. Let them know that everyone deals with trauma in a different way. You have no expectation of how much time it should take or how they should behave. Assure them that whatever it takes, you'll be there with them through it.

DON'T

Don't be critical or judgmental. Don't say things like, "This wouldn't have happened if..." "There must be sin in your life." "You're not trusting God with your feelings."[2]

♥

Caring People Need to Be Organized

Caring people need to have the basic tools to be organized. There needs to be a place where all of the pertinent information is stored, where in a moment's notice information can be written and retrieved. Certain tools that I have found invaluable are:

- A 5½″ x 8½″ three-ring-binder notebook
- A year's calendar
- A month-on-a-page calendar
- A daily-schedule calendar
- Colored divider tabs

This basic notebook can become your lifeline to your care ministry. It will contain all the pertinent information for your ministry. These tools can be obtained from your local office supply store, or we can furnish them to you simply by writing to our office. Request a price list of materials. See page 6 for information.

Your calendars become the backbone of your scheduling. At one simple glance you can quickly see where you need to be and what needs to be done.

A Year's Calendar and Month-on-a-Page Calendar

These two calendars can be incorporated into one calendar that serves both needs. I have even gone one step farther and used colored felt-tip markers to help me quickly identify, through color coding, specific areas of my life:

- Purple—CARE Committee Activities
- Yellow—Children Activities
- Orange—Family Activities
- Blue—Church Activities

By a simple glance at the month, I readily know where I'm to be. We have a motto in our home which states: "If I fail to plan, I plan to fail." Nothing happens without proper planning. It might take a little extra time up front, but planning saves many precious minutes in the end. Planning time is the key to your success. There is usually a correlation between the amount of time you plan and how successful an event will become. *Big planning gives big success. Little planning gives little success.*

Exhibit F (page 178) shows how a typical calendar might look in your notebook.

A Daily-Schedule Calendar

Our month-at-a-glance calendar doesn't provide enough room to list all the 30-minute segments in your day. This is where the daily calendar becomes so helpful. You can break your day into manageable parts. Many times we have the tendency to crowd too much into our calendar, and we become rushed as we go from one activity to another. I have a simple formula for allowing the proper time for events on my daily calendar.

If I have been to this place before, I allow one-quarter more time than I think I might need to for the appointment. For example, if I think I need one hour, I will block out one hour and 15 minutes on my calendar. If I have never been to this place before, I will allow one half more time than I think I might need. For example, if I think I need one hour, I will block out one hour and 30 minutes.

This formula has really been helpful to me. It allows for emergencies, heavy traffic, detours, gas station pit stops, etc. More important than that, it greatly reduces your stress and your family will find you more fun to be around.

Colored Divider Tabs

Whenever possible, I use color in my notebook. It's more exciting. Sure, clear and manila-colored dividers are less

JULY 1990

SUNDAY	MONDAY	TUESDAY	WEDNESDAY	THURSDAY	FRIDAY	SATURDAY
30	31					1 — Joe & Ann Mobley #1-683-2607 Jones cooking
2 — Joe & Ann Mobley #2 683-2607 Levin's cooking	3 — Joe & Ann Mobley #3 683-2607 DeLorenzo's cooking	4 — Joe & Ann Mobley #4 683-2007 Merrihew's cooking	5 — visit Jane Brown @ Parkview Hospital	6 — Care Group Planning Committee 9:30-11:30	7 — visit Jane Brown @ hospital	8 — Ricky Sims #2 meal 683-5426 Wilmot's cooking
9 — Ricky Sims #4 meal 683-5426 Davis' cooking	10 — send get well card to Mary Ellen	11 — Mary Peters #1 meal 625-5101	12 — Mary Peters #3 meal 625-5101 Abbott's	13 — Mary Peters #2 meal 625-5101 Beall's cooking	14 — Visit Mary Peters. Call first.	15 — Jackie Joiner admission to Riverside Clinic
16 — Visit Jackie Joiner - minor surgery	17 — Jackie Joiner #1 meal Russell's cooking 720-1888	18 — Jackie Joiner #2 meal 728-1889 Davies cooking	19 — Mary Blooms funeral Olivewood 11:30am	20 — Gerri Jackson c-section Community Hospital 10AM	21	22 — Gerri Jackson comes home #4 meal Brown's cooking
23	24	25 — J Billie Conn's family lunch-only Patti Wayken	26	27 — visit Timmy Matthews @ Parkview Hospital	28	29 — Courtney family lunch soup & salad Jones cooking

expensive, but they don't have that extra bounce which makes life so much fun. When given a choice, go with bright colors. They will make you a more cheerful person.

I use a couple of sets of three- or five-notched divider tabs. With these you can readily divide up the various sections in your notebook so you can quickly turn to the proper sections. This will save you a lot of time thumbing through the pages. In addition, you can expand and add new sections to your notebook.

In our CARE notebook we had several added sections which gave fingertip data to help facilitate meeting people's needs. The added sections were:

- Address Book
- Items Loaned/Borrowed
- Expenses Record
- Sources and Resources List
- Prayer Requests List
- Weekly Menus
- Shopping List
- Dishes Suitable for Crisis Calls
- Notes

Address Book

An inexpensive section of pages divided from A–Z will give you immediate retrieval of important data. This address book will save you a lot of calls to the information operator and time spent consulting the local phone directory. Write in the addresses and telephone numbers in pencil; that way changes can be made easily if and when needed.

ADDRESSES

Barnes, Brad 417 23rd St. Manhattan Beach, CA 90266	*Home* *Work*	213 / 547-8126 213 / 437-4513 /
Beck, Bill & Susan 2212 Broadmore Newport Beach, CA 92060	*Home* *Work*	714 / 754-0392 714 / 624-0261 /
Brogger, Bob & Yoli 2469 Bison Newport Beach, CA 92060	*Home* *Work*	714 / 649-6830 714 / 646-5417 /
Bueler, John & Barbara P.O. Box 627A Cedar Ridge Park, CA 92311	*Home* *Work*	714 / 327-4244 714 / 327-4121 /
	Home *Work*	/ / /
	Home *Work*	/ / /
	Home *Work*	/ / /
	Home *Work*	/ / /

Important Numbers

Another form that can go on a page or two after your address book is a listing of often-used telephone numbers of important people. Many times I don't need an address, city, or zip code, so I use this listing. It saves time, energy, and stress.

Items Loaned/Borrowed

How many times have you tried to remember who you loaned that card table, serving tray, crystal pitcher, cookbook, or saucepan to, but your mind draws a blank and you just can't remember? Yes, I was no different at one time—until I misplaced several valuable items (to this day I have not gotten them back). I am sure they are being used by wonderful, warm, friendly people who can't remember where they borrowed the items from. They just showed up after a party at their home or after asking if they could use the item for a special occasion.

I designed this form to help me keep track of items which I loaned or borrowed. I found it only takes a few seconds to write down the particulars in my notebook.

If you are taking a casserole dish to a shut-in, you might tell them that you will be back in a few days to pick up the dish. Or if you have some goodies in a beautiful love basket, you might tell the recipient that the contents are theirs and you will be by on Friday to pick up the basket.

It takes 21 days to learn a new habit. The habit of keeping track of loaned/borrowed items will save you a lot of valuable time and money figuring out who has what.

Expenses Record

Keeping track of expenses is always a concern for those who work on a CARE committee. We all know that many times we act out of love and concern and don't expect to be

IMPORTANT NUMBERS

Service Person	Phone Number	Service Person	Phone Number
Ambulance	555-4203	Neighbor —Sally	555-0011
Appliance Repair	555-4219	Newspaper	555-4738
Dentist — Merrihew	555-4703	Orthodontist	555-1104
Doctor —Turnbull	555-4909	Pastor	555-0767
Electrician —Rusty	555-1001	Poison Control	555-0013
Fire	555-9996	Police	555-5001
Gardener —Mike	555-4618	Pool Service	—
Gas Co. Emergency	555-5551	Plumber	555-0114
Glass Repair		School(s) — Elem.	555-9013
Heating/Air Conditioning Repair Person	555-0013	School(s) — Jr. High	555-1111
Husband's Work	555-0321	Veterinarian	—
Insurance (Car)	555-0112	Cat's Name	Tiger
Insurance (Home)	555-0112	Dog's Name	Mickie
		Animal Control	555-0014
		Security System	555-1163
		Trash	555-0731
		Newspaper-Boy	555-0014

ITEMS LOANED/BORROWED

Month/Year July, 1990

Date	Item	Who	Returned
7/1	platter	Brown's	7/3
7/1	book	Cheryl C.	
7/3	cookbook	Kathy P.	7/9
7/6	mixer	Barb D.	7/10
7/6	card table	church	
7/10	sauce pan	Julie M.	7/15
7/12	camera	Jenny M.	
7/13	lantern	Joe B.	7/16
7/16	flashlight	Billy R.	
7/20	card table	Dryer's	7/25
7/22	book	Betty B.	
7/24	table cloth	Jane M.	7/28
7/27	American flag	Jill B.	
7/30	portable stove	David B.	

repaid. Our pastor and board of elders wanted to make sure that this ministry was sponsored and supported by the church's leadership. A line item for our CARE committee was added to the church budget and we were responsible for staying within our budget allocations.

Each of the ladies on our committee was given an "Expense" form each month (see Exhibit J on page 185) and was requested to keep a running record of all authorized expenses. We attached a letter-sized envelope on the back of this form so all receipts could be kept. At the end of the month, each committee member forwarded the form and envelope to our committee chairperson for her approval and forwarding to our church office for reimbursement.

Many of the women used this form for their own record-keeping within the home. They were amazed how writing down a record of all expenditures made them aware of actual costs for living. When they and their husbands reviewed their budgets for the month, they had a visual record of where their money went. They could quickly decide which kind of expenditures they would eliminate in the next month's purchases.

If your family has a difficult time staying within your budget, you might want to try this technique. It has proven to be very valuable in working with singles and couples who have financial problems. Our monthly goal should be to spend less than we earn. Only in this way can we be responsible financially to our Lord.

Sources and Resources

Have you ever scratched your head and asked yourself, "What is the name of the florist which gave us such good flowers last time?" Many times we spend unnecessary time trying to flip through the Yellow Pages of our telephone book or our own address book. One way to eliminate this problem is to create listings by grouping phone numbers of similar sources together (such as bakeries, counselors,

EXPENSES

Month/Year July, 1990

Date	Item	Method of Payment	Amount	
7/1	flowers for Sally	check	20	—
7/1	babysitting - Jones	✓	5	—
7/2	paper goods - Abels	✓	6	27
7/5	cup - Nelsons	✓	4	38
7/7	Love Basket - Pete's	✓	14	15
7/9	Sympathy cards	✓	7	16
7/10	food - Dryer's	✓	21	14
7/11	cookies - reception	✓	22	—
7/14	rental of coffee pot	✓	6	—
7/15	food - Lowry's	✓	22	14
7/17	flowers - Peter's	✓	10	—
7/19	telephone calls	✓	6	24
7/25	paper goods	✓	10	25
7/30	gas mileage	✓	7	50
		Total		

doctors, florists, attorneys, abuse centers, etc.). We created our form called "Sources and Resources" and added this section to our notebook. It became very valuable in keeping apples with apples. We found that as we shared these organizational tools with our ladies, they were getting their personal lives more organized. They expanded this form to include headings such as: theaters, nursery schools, clothing stores, churches, insurance agencies, stockbrokers, and real estate brokers.

Some of the ladies commented, "I didn't realize how being organized would really save me a lot of time. Now I can do things I never had time to do before."

I have found that if you give yourself 15 minutes a day to spend on better organization, you will be amazed at the compounded benefits it gives you and your family. (See Exhibit K on page 187.)

Prayer Requests List

> Any hour when helping others
> Or when bearing heavy care,
> Is the time to call our Father;
> It's the proper time for prayer.
> —Zimmerman

"Those who do not pray as much as they could, do not pray as much as they should."[3]

We must not limit our prayerful conversations to those special "calls" known as devotions, essential as they are. Paul said, "Pray without ceasing" (1 Thessalonians 5:17 NASB). We need to take greater advantage of that marvelous two-way communication system by remaining open to God and by calling on Him anytime, anywhere.

The CARE committee ladies soon began to realize that they could not rely on their own resources, but had to reach out to God and ask for wisdom, energy, enthusiasm, and guidance. This gave us a great opportunity to spend

Category: FLORISTS

Name/Address Shaffer's · 687-5363
4898 La Sierra
Riverside, CA 92517

Notes medium price range - prompt delivery

Name/Address Arlington · 689-5291
9687 Magnolia
Arlington, CA 92509

Notes Christian family - creative design

Name/Address Flower Loft · 787-8720
3697 Arlington
Riverside, CA 92507

Notes Excellent quality - prompt delivery
talk to Ann

Name/Address Anna's · 682-5525
2619 University
Riverside, CA 92506

Notes good - fair prices
talk to Kim

Name/Address

Notes

time with our ladies in prayer for those who were directed to us for a special ministry. "How can I keep track of all the various prayer requests? I put them on a piece of paper and I lose the paper and I forget to pray for those needs. What can be done? Please help to organize my cluttered mind and record keeping." Have you ever had a similar dilemma in keeping track of your prayer requests? We designed a very simple form which kept track of those requests.

At church we got requests, over the phone we got requests, at the grocery store we got requests, at our child's school's open house we got requests—we even got requests in our pastor's sermons.

Just listen, listen, listen, and you will hear of hurting people's prayer needs. What do you do when you hear these requests? Just turn to your tidy notebook, turn to your "Prayer Request" tab, and make another entry to your ever growing "needs" list. Our women became excited as they saw how God worked in dealing with all of our prayer requests. We soon realized that all of our prayers weren't answered by a favorable "yes." People did die, couples did get divorced, and cancer wasn't always cured, but we did begin to realize that God was sovereign and He had a master plan for all of our lives. Our ladies truly grew as their prayer life became more disciplined.

Not only did their lists include requests from the CARE committee, but they also began to reflect their own family and personal requests. If you can't keep track of your prayer needs, you, too, might want to try this way of becoming organized in your prayer life (see Exhibit L).

For more information regarding a more organized prayer life, refer to my book, *More Hours in My Day*, published by Harvest House. I have an excellent chapter on "Prayer Organization" on pages 193-204.

> *Seven days without*
> *prayer makes one weak*

PRAYER REQUESTS

Date	Request	Scripture	Update/Answer	Date
7/1	Evelyn's mother's surgery		all's well	7/3
7/1	Kevin's graduation		with honors	7/1
7/3	the Field's baby		much better	7/6
7/5	Grandma's hospital stay		improving released	7/8 7/10
7/7	Jennifer's tooth		pulled	7/9
7/8	Brad's Escrow	Phil. 4:19	closed	7/9
7/9	Craig's home loan	Matt. 6:8	reapplied approved	7/12 7/25
7/12	Aunt Gladys' funeral		great to be a Christian	7/12
7/20	Pastor Foor is sick		preached on Sunday	7/24
7/21	Inter-varsity committee			
7/23	Bevan's fever		down to normal	7/25
7/25	Christine's 1st date		she was so pretty	7/27
7/28	Chad's summer league tryout		he made the team	7/29
7/30	Phil Jackson's surgery		not doing well	

Weekly Menus

This is the area where Sue Gregg really had a valuable contribution to make. Her gift is menu planning, developing shopping lists, and designing health-oriented recipes. Sue is a graduate home economist who has a real passion for designing food that will enhance a prolonged lifestyle. Her skills and food knowledge gave our committee an invaluable resource for making sure that our food needs would be above average. Again, this opportunity and need gave Sue and me a way to teach our ladies a little bit of proper nutrition. Many questions came out of these sessions. Not only did the families with food needs become enriched, so did the families of our committee ladies.

We wanted to emphasize foods that were high in fiber, low in sodium, low in fats, low in cholesterol, and high in taste. This was not an easy task because most recipes we find in cookbooks, magazines, and newspapers are just the opposite. The American diet is one of the leading causes of heart attacks in our society. Our food kills our families.

Sue went to work and customized basic recipes that our ladies could make in their own kitchens by using standard items that could be found in their own grocery stores. We didn't want them to have to go to health-food stores to get little or unknown ingredients.

The "Weekly Menus" became a great way to plan and chart the meals that we would provide for each family. Each schedule was individually planned for the specific needs of the person(s) that needed meals. In most cases we found that the evening meal was the one that was needed.

Occasionally our ladies did provide breakfasts and lunches. When they did, they used recipes from our *Busy Woman's Breakfast Book* and *Busy Woman's Lunch and Snacks Book*. These meals met our high standards and also featured ease of preparation.

Our ladies transferred use of the "Weekly Menus" form from the CARE committee to home. We gave them a plan

WEEKLY MENUS

Date July 3, 1990

Day of week	Breakfast	Lunch	Dinner
Monday			Mobley's #2 menu soup & salad
Tuesday			Mobley's #3 menu soup & salad w/muffins
Wednesday			Mobley's #4 menu tamale pie
Thursday			
Friday			
Saturday			
Sunday			Ricky Sims #2 menu soup & salad

and it works. Where our ladies procrastinated about planning for their families' meals, they found they were totally frustrated in getting meals together. Many ladies tried to short-circuit the system and ended up succumbing to the fast-food dilemma. By preplanning there was less frustration, saving of time in the markets, saving of money at the register, and happier families.

One of the ladies who attended one of my seminars wrote a letter stating she gave her son on his seventh birthday the option of going out to eat at any place he would select or to have Mom cook his favorite meal at home. Her son said, "Mom, could we stay home with the rest of the family?" Mom was so touched that he wanted to stay home and enjoy her cooking. This gave one mom encouragement to upgrade her domestic skills and make home an increasingly good place to eat.

Shopping List

After selecting the menu, the next step is to go over your shopping list and select the items you will need to purchase at the market. This list has been revised by many ladies to go along with their own market. This is certainly an excellent time-saver and reduces the amount of time you spend in the market. Research has proven that after 30 minutes in the market, you will spend 75 cents for every minute you remain in the market.

Another advantage of using the shopping list is that you will become disciplined to only purchase what's on the list. We have had ladies comment that they save anywhere from 14 to 20 dollars a week by sticking to what's on the list. I recommend that you don't take your children with you when you shop. It's amazing how TV commercials influence our children. Commercials somehow convince children to request food that you've never even heard of. Childless shopping will save money.

SHOPPING LIST

Date 7/1/90

Qty.

Staples
_____ Cereal
_____ Flour
_____ Jello
_____ Mixes
_____ Nuts
_____ Stuffing
_____ Sugar

Spices
_____ Bacon Bits
_____ Baking Powder
_____ Chocolate
_____ Coconut
___1___ Salt/Pepper
_____ Soda

Pasta
_____ Inst. Potato
___1___ Mixes
___1___ Pasta
___1___ Rice
_____ Spaghetti

Drinks
___1___ Apple Cider
_____ Coffee
___1___ Juice
_____ Sparkling
_____ Tea

Canned Goods
___1___ Canned Fruit
Strawberry
___1___ beans
_____
_____
_____ Canned Meals
_____ Canned Meat
_____ Canned Vegetables
_____
_____ Soups
___1___ chicken
___2___ Tuna

Qty.

Condiments
___1___ Catsup
_____ Honey
_____ Jelly/Jam
_____ Mayonnaise
_____ Molassas
_____ Mustard
_____ Oil
_____ Peanut Butter
_____ Pickles
_____ Relish
___1___ Salad Dressing
_____ Shortening
___1___ Syrup
___1___ Tomato Paste
_____ Tomato Sauce
___1___ Vinegar

Paper Goods
_____ Foil
_____ Napkins
_____ Paper Towels
_____ Plastic Wrap
_____ Tissues
_____ Toilet Paper
_____ Toothpicks
_____ Trash Bags
___1___ Waxed Paper
_____ Zip Bags
_____ Small
___1___ Large

Household
_____ Bleach
_____ Laundry Soap
_____ Dish Soap
_____ Dishwasher Soap
_____ Fabric Softener
_____ Furniture Polish
_____ Light Bulbs
_____ Pet Food
_____ Vacuum Bags
_____
_____
_____

Qty.

Fresh Produce
_____ Fruit
___1___ apple
_____
_____ Vegetables
___1___ celery
___1___ lettuce

Personal Items
_____ Body Soap
_____ Deodorant
_____ Fem. Protection
_____ Hair Care
_____ Makeup

Frozen Food
_____ Ice Cream
___1___ yogurt
_____ Juice
_____ T.V. Dinners
_____ Vegetables
_____

Pastry
___1___ Bread/s
_____ Buns
_____ Chips
_____ Cookies
___1___ Crackers
_____ Croutons

Meat
_____ Beef
___1___ Chicken

Dairy
___1___ Butter
_____ Cheese
_____ Cottage Cheese
_____ Eggs
___1___ Milk
_____ Sour Cream
_____

As our daughter, Jenny, became a teenager, she loved to drive the car to do my shopping; in fact, she would have done anything to drive my car. Jenny also began to help with menu selection and making out the shopping list—a great teaching experience between mother and daughter.

The ladies on the CARE committee found this shopping list very valuable in meal preparation. Many ladies made out one shopping list for the CARE needs and one for their own menus. Another little trick is to attach the Shopping List and grocery receipt to an Expenses form—all set for reimbursement.

Dishes Suitable for Crisis Calls

The following recipes have been selected for high nutritional value, ease of preparation, economy, and high taste values. Casseroles are easy to prepare ahead of time and freeze for quick delivery to a needy person(s).

———————— ♥ ————————

You cannot depend on others
for your self-worth.
It must come from
within—through God.

THE COMPLETE CRISIS CALL MENU

BASIC MENU	EATING BETTER LIFESTYLE TIPS	REFERENCE
Main Dish	*Make with:* whole grains such as brown rice, whole grain pastas, ground turkey, skinned chicken, natural cheddar cheeses, fresh or frozen vegetables, reduced fat and salt vegetables, reduced fat and salt.	*The Busy Woman's Main Dish Book* *The Busy Woman's Soup Book*
Vegetable	*First choice:* fresh *Second choice:* frozen—without salt. Try to avoid canned vegetables.	*The Busy Woman's Main Dish Book*
Salad	*First choice:* dark, leafy lettuce mixed with iceberg lettuce and several fresh vegetables. *Second choice (if no fresh ingredients on hand):* molded salad prepared with real fruit juice, honey, and unflavored gelatin. *Dressings:* olive oil and vinegar or lemon juice; yogurt or buttermilk types; commercial dressings without sugar or chemicals; serve separately from salad.	*The Busy Woman's Main Dish Book*
Muffin or Bread	*Make with:* whole grain flour (use unbleached white flour or part unbleached white flour as second choice); honey; without fat or cut amount in half when using butter or oil; avoid vegetable shortening.	*The Busy Woman's Muffin Book* *The Busy Woman's Soup Book*
Dessert (optional)	*Make with:* whole grains or whole-grain flours, fresh fruits, honey; reduce amount of butter or oil; avoid shortening; avoid commercially prepared desserts with lots of chemicals, white flour, and white sugar.	*The Busy Woman's Breakfast Book* *Eating Better Desserts*

♡ **Crisis Call Menu #1** ♡

Creole Black-eyed Peas 'n Corn
Minute Bran Muffins
Orange Tossed or *Tossed Salad* or
Pineapple Sunshine Mold

Pantry Supply List
(fresh ingredients not included)

Creole Black-eyed Peas 'n Corn

2 cups (1 lb.) dry black-eyed peas
Bay leaves
Italian seasoning
Butter
Rosemary
1 lb. can stewed tomatoes
8-oz. can tomato sauce
Honey
Salt
10 oz. frozen corn (freezer)

Minute Bran Muffins:

1/2 cup raisins (optional)
1 1/2 cups unprocessed wheat bran (Miller's)
Honey
1 1/2 cups whole wheat or whole wheat pastry flour
Baking soda
Salt
Walnuts (optional)
Muffin papers (optional)

Pineapple Sunshine Mold:

1 1/2 pkg. unflavored gelatin (1 Tbsp.)

6-oz. can unsweetened pineapple juice
Honey
8-oz. can unsweetened crushed pineapple
1/4 cup chopped nuts (optional)—almonds, walnuts, or pecans
6-oz. can frozen orange juice (freezer)

For main dish, salad, and muffins:

Small jar honey (or 2/3 cup)

♡ Crisis Call Menu #2 ♡

Spring Garden Special
Tossed Salad
Lemon Ginger Muffins
Yogurt Pie (optional)

Pantry Supply List
(fresh ingredients not included)

Spring Garden Special:

Garlic, 2 cloves
1/2 cup minced parsley
Butter
Salt
6 cups vegetable soup stock (or use water)
2 28-oz. cans whole tomatoes
Bernard Jensen's Natural Vegetable Seasoning (optional)
10-oz. pkg. frozen French-cut green beans (freezer)

Fresh vegetables called for in recipe are commonly available in most kitchens; if not, any fresh vegetables on hand can be used.

Lemon Ginger Muffins:

(These muffins are tastier prepared with fresh lemon peel and fresh ginger, but dried ingredients are listed for emergencies).

> 2 cups whole wheat pastry flour
> 1 cup plain yogurt or buttermilk
> ¼ cup lemon juice
> 2 Tbsp. lemon peel (fresh preferred)
> ½ cup honey
> Baking soda
> Butter
> 2 Tbsp. chopped ginger (fresh preferred)

Note: Fresh ginger will keep almost indefinitely when cut in small pieces and covered with dry sherry or white wine in a covered glass jar in refrigerator. Rinse well and peel (if desired) to use.

Yogurt Pie:

> Graham crackers (whole wheat preferred)
> Butter
> 1 Tbsp. granulated fructose (sugar may be
> ⠀⠀substituted, using 2 Tbsp. in recipe)
> 8-oz. can unsweetened crushed pineapple
> 2 pkgs. unflavored gelatin
> ¼ cup honey
> 3 cups lowfat yogurt
> Vanilla extract

♡ Crisis Call Menu #3 ♡

Brown Rice Pilaf ⠀⠀⠀ *Broccoli or*
Carrots Hawaiian or Frozen Peas
Tossed Salad or Spinach Salad
Minute Bran or Lemon-Ginger Muffins

Pantry Supply List
(fresh ingredients not included)

Brown Rice Pilaf with chicken added:

2 cans (3 cups) chicken broth (or chicken bouillon cubes, or prepare broth while cooking chicken)

1¼ cups long grain brown rice

¼ cup whole wheat kernels or wild rice (or ¼ cup more brown rice)

¼ cup almonds

Chicken broth

Worcestershire sauce (variation, optional)

Sue's "Kitchen Magic" seasoning (or chicken broth)

Parsley

Chives

Bernard Jensen's Natural Vegetable Seasoning (variation, optional)
(optional, if available)

1 to 2 cups chopped cooked chicken or ½ to 1 lb. to cook and chop (freezer)

Carrots Hawaiian:

8-oz. can pineapple tidbits

Honey

Lemon juice (fresh preferred)

Salt

Butter

Frozen Peas:

10 oz. green peas (freezer)

Muffins:

See Crisis Call Menu #1 and #2

♡ **Crisis Call Menu #4** ♡

Favorite Tamale Pie
Tossed Salad or Spinach Salad
Orange Tossed Salad
with
Sweet Mayonnaise Dressing or
Sweet Lite Dressing
(substitute canned peaches if
fresh oranges unavailable)

Pantry Supply List
(fresh ingredients not included)

Favorite Tamalie Pie:

>   1 lb. seasoned ground turkey (freezer)
>   2 cups tomato, spaghetti, or pasta sauce
>   10 oz. (2 cups) frozen corn (freezer)
>   2¼-oz. can sliced ripe olives
>   Chili powder
>   Cut garlic or garlic powder
>   ¼ lb. (1 cup) cornmeal (stoneground preferred)—store in refrigerator or freezer
>   Butter
>   Salt

Sweet Mayonnaise Dressing:

>   ¼ c. mayonnaise
>   ¼ c. nonfat plain yogurt
>   1½ tsp. lemon juice
>   1½ tsp. crystalline fructose or honey

Sweet Lite Dressing

>   2 tsp. crystalline fructose or honey
>   2 tsp. lemon juice
>   ⅛ tsp. salt

♡ Crisis Call Menu #5 ♡

> *Tuna Noodle Yummy*
> *Tossed, Spinach,* or
> *Orange Tossed Salad*
> *Pineapple Sunshine Mold* or
> *Broccoli* or
> *Carrots Hawaiian* or *Frozen Peas*
> *Minute Bran Muffins* or
> *Lemon-Ginger Muffins*

Pantry Supply List
(fresh ingredients not included)

Tuna Noodle Yummy:

>   Salt
>   Olive oil
>   8-oz. package noodles (whole grain preferred)
>   1 cup nonfat plain yogurt
>   ½ cup sour cream (light)
>   Garlic powder
>   Parmesan cheese
>   2 Tbsp. flour (whole wheat pastry preferred)
>   6½-oz. can tuna, water pack (50% less salt preferred)
>   ½ cup frozen peas (freezer)
>   Almonds (optional)

Pineapple Sunshine Mold:

　　See Crisis Call Menu #1

Carrots Hawaiian:
(serve with green salad, but not with Pineapple Sunshine Mold)

　　See Crisis Call Menu #3

Frozen Peas:
(if not used in main dish)

　　large bag frozen peas (freezer)—take out amount needed for size family you're serving

Minute Bran or *Lemon-Ginger Muffins:*

　　See Crisis Call Menu #1 or #2

Creole Black-eyed Peas 'n Corn

Amount: 6 to 8 Servings (8–9 cups or 2½ qt. casserole)

1. Soak peas in water 1 to 3 hours or overnight:
   2 cups (1 lb.) black-eyed peas
   8 cups water

2. Bring peas in water to a boil, add seasonings and boil 3 minutes; reduce heat to simmer:
   1 bay leaf
   1 tsp. Italian Seasoning
   ½ tsp. rosemary

3. Sauté vegetables in butter (optional for best flavor) or add unsautéed vegetables directly to the peas as they cook:
   2 Tbsp. butter, melted (optional for sautéing)

    1 onion, chopped
    1 green pepper, chopped

4. Continue to cook until peas are almost tender, about 1½ hours. Add more water, if needed.

5. Add remaining ingredients, stirring in the corn after casserole cools completely, just before freezing:
    1 lb. can stewed tomatoes
    8-oz. can tomato sauce
    ½ stick (¼ cup) butter
    2 Tbsp. honey
    ½ tsp. salt
    1½ cups frozen corn

6. To reheat, turn frozen casserole out into a saucepan over direct low heat. Add a couple cups of water. When heat has thawed the dish completely, bring to a boil, lower to simmering and simmer 30 minutes. Add more water as needed. Recipe should be quite soupy. Remove bay leaf before serving.

Per serving (of 8) with vegetables sautéed in butter: 296 cal., 12 gr. protein, 10 gr. fat (29%), 6 gr. dietary fiber

Per serving (of 8) without sautéing vegetables in butter: 270 cal., 7 gm. fat (23%)

Minute Bran Muffins

Our classic family favorite from which all the other muffin recipes were developed. These go with everything! Serve warm or cold.

Amount: 10-12 large

1. Preheat oven at 350°.

2. Grease muffin pan.

3. Cover with warm water and let stand 5 to 10 minutes:
   ½ cup raisins (optional)

4. Blend together and let stand for 5 minutes:
   ½ cup boiling water
   1½ cups unprocessed wheat bran (Miller's)

5. Blend together thoroughly in order given with wire whisk:
   1 egg
   ¼ to ⅓ cup honey
   1 cup buttermilk or sour milk
   Bran mixture

6. Blend dry ingredients together in separate bowl:
   1½ cups whole wheat or whole wheat
      pastry flour
   1¼ tsp. soda
   1 tsp. salt
   ½ cup walnuts, chopped (optional)

7. Blend drained raisins, then dry ingredients into liquid ingredients just until mixed. Do not overmix!

8. Fill muffin cups almost full and bake 20 to 25 minutes.

9. Cool 5 to 10 minutes before removing from pan.

Variations for allergies: Substitute ¼ cup tofu for 1 egg, blending it with other liquids in the blender.

Substitute unsweetened apple or pineapple juice for buttermilk. Use the same amount.

(For additional ordering information regarding The Busy Women's Cookbooks, see page 6.)

Orange Tossed Salad

I serve this often, usually with only oranges and 1 or 2 other ingredients tossed with greens.

1. With greens as the main ingredient, toss with oranges and 1 or more of remaining ingredients, as desired:
   iceberg lettuce, torn
   dark leafy lettuce and/or ruby red, torn
   oranges, peeled, chopped
   pineapple, chopped fresh, or canned chunks
     or tidbits
   bananas, peeled, sliced
   apple, green or red, unpeeled chopped
   carrots, grated
   celery, chopped or diagonally sliced

2. Suggested dressings: *Sweet Mayonnaise* or *Sweet Lite*.

Sweet Mayonnaise Dressing

Amount: ¹/₂ Cup

1. Blend thoroughly with wire whisk:
   ¹/₄ cup mayonnaise (such as Hollywood brand)
   ¹/₄ cup nonfat plain yogurt
   1¹/₂ tsp. lemon juice
   1¹/₂ tsp. crystalline fructose or honey

Per 1 Tbsp.: 1.25 fat, 62 cal., 6 gm. fat (88%), 44 mg. sodium

Sweet Lite Dressing

Amount: ¹/₄ Cup

1. Blend with wire whisk thoroughly:
   ¹/₄ cup nonfat yogurt
   2 tsp. crystalline fructose or honey

2 tsp. lemon juice
⅛ tsp. salt

Per 1 Tbsp.: 15 cal., 1 gm. protein (21%), 3 gm. carbohydrate (78%), 75 mg. sodium

Spring Garden Special

This is a favorite soup we serve as the first course for banquets.

Amount: 15 Servings

1. Melt in frying pan for sautéing vegetables:
   ¼ cup butter

2. Add and sauté until soft:
   1 large onion, chopped
   2 cups chopped celery
   2 cloves garlic, minced

3. Bring to boil in soup pot:
   6 cups water or vegetable soup stock
   2 28-oz. cans (7 cups) whole tomatoes

4. Add to soup pot:
   2 cups thin carrot rounds
   2 cups diced potatoes, peeled or unpeeled
   Sautéed vegetables

5. Reduce heat and simmer until carrots and potatoes are tender, about 20 to 30 minutes.

6. Add:
   10-oz. package frozen French cut green beans
   1 or 2 small zucchini, unpeeled and sliced (optional)
   ½ cup minced parsley
   1 to 2 Tbsp. Bernard Jensen's Natural
      Vegetable Seasoning, to taste
   1 tsp. salt, to taste

7. Simmer 5 minutes or longer to cook zucchini and beans. and blend seasonings.

Reduced Fat Variation: Omit sautéing of vegetables in butter. Add onion, celery, and garlic to soup with carrots and potatoes.

Lemon-Ginger Muffins

A deliciously light muffin that compliments soups and main dishes.

Amount: 10 large or 12 medium

1. Preheat oven to 375°.

2. Grease muffin pan (muffin papers are not suitable for this recipe).

3. Prepare and set aside:
     2 Tbsp. fresh grated lemon peel
     2 Tbsp. chopped fresh ginger*

4. Blend together and let stand (mixture will foam up):
     1 cup plain yogurt or buttermilk
     1 tsp. baking soda

5. Blend well in a separate bowl:
     ¼ cup soft butter (optional)
     ½ cup honey

6. Add to honey-butter, blending in thoroughly.
     2 large eggs
     Grated lemon and chopped ginger

---

* To preserve fresh ginger: cut in small pieces, place in jar, and cover with dry sherry or white wine. Cover tightly and refrigerate.

7. Mix into honey-egg mixture alternately with the yogurt or buttermilk:
    2 cups whole wheat pastry flour (mix in ⅔ cup at a time)

8. Fill muffin cups almost full. If making 10 large muffins, fill two center cups with water.

9. Bake 18 to 20 minutes.

10. While muffins bake, mix together:
    ¼ cup lemon juice
    1 Tbsp. honey or granulated fructose

11. Cool muffins 5 minutes. Dip top and bottom of each muffin in lemon juice mixture.

Yogurt Pie

A light dessert for a fun breakfast—prepare the day before.

Amount: 9 Servings

1. Make graham cracker crust by blending together:
    1 generous cup whole wheat graham cracker crumbs* (6 crackers)
    ¼ cup melted butter
    1 Tbsp. granulated fructose

2. Pat crumbs into bottom of 9″ x 9″ cake pan. Chill in freezer 10 minutes.

---

*Buy whole wheat graham crackers at health food store. Mi-Del is a tasty brand. These have no preservatives and go rancid if stored very long—freeze crackers kept longer than 2 weeks. If you buy honey grahams at supermarket, be sure to read the ingredients label first!

3. Bake 10 to 12 minutes at 350°.

4. Drain thoroughly, reserving juice:
   8-oz. can crushed pineapple, unsweetened

5. Blend together and let stand 5 minutes:
   Drained pineapple juice (about ⅓ cup)
   2 packages unflavored gelatin

6. Dissolve the gelatin over medium heat, stirring constantly.

7. Remove from heat and blend in:
   ¼ cup honey

8. In mixing bowl blend together well with wire whisk:
   3 cups lowfat yogurt
   1½ tsp. vanilla
   Crushed pineapple (about ¾ cup from can)
   Dissolved gelatin in juice

9. Pour into graham cracker crust and chill until set in refrigerator.

10. Score servings, 3 x 3, and garnish each serving with:
    ½ fresh strawberry
    2 half-slices kiwi fruit

Brown Rice Pilaf

One of our company recipe favorites with *Baked Parmesan Chicken*. Especially flavorful with *Sue's "Kitchen Magic" Seasoning*. For a second meal I often add bits of leftover chicken and freeze it for a complete "dinner's ready" main dish.

Amount: 4¹/₂ Cups (serves 6)

1. Place in a saucepan that has a tight-fitting lid, bring to boil and boil uncovered for 5 minutes:

    1¹/₄ cups long grain brown rice (see note following directions)
    ¹/₄ cup whole wheat kernels (health food store) or wild rice (or ¹/₄ cup more brown rice)
    ¹/₄ cup slivered or chopped almonds
    3 cups water or chicken broth
    4 tsp. Sue's "Kitchen Magic" Seasoning (use chicken broth if you do not have this seasoning)
    2 tsp. Worcestershire sauce (Kikkoman Lite preferred, or Liquid Aminos)

2. Cover with tight-fitting lid, reduce heat to very low and simmer 50 to 60 minutes or until all the water is absorbed and rice is tender. Do not remove lid or stir during cooking as this tends to produce sticky rice.

3. While rice cooks lightly sauté 2 chopped green onions for a minute or two in 1 or 2 Tbsp. water.

4. Fold green onions into rice just before serving. Fresh chopped parsley or freeze-dried or fresh chives can be used in place of green onions.

Per ³/₄ cup serving (long grain)
   Exchanges: 1 fat, 2.5 bread; 207 cal., 5.5 gm. protein (11%), 4 gm. fat (16%), 38 gm. carbohydrate (73%), 3 gm. dietary fiber, 498 mg. sodium

Variation.

Brown Rice Pilaf recipe variation calls for chicken broth in place of Worcestershire sauce and Bernard Jensen's Natural Vegetable Seasoning. Chicken broth is generally easier to obtain and keep available in a pantry supply. Add cooked chicken to the pilaf after it is cooked to make a heartier dish or prepare chicken separately such as Baked Parmesan Chicken, Chicken Paprikish, or Yaki Tori Chicken—all tasty recipes from *The Busy Woman's Main Dish Book.*

Note: There are many varieties of brown rice. The most common are short grain, medium grain, and long grain. Long grain brown rice is less sticky or chewy in texture than short or medium grain rice. Most people who are accustomed to eating fluffy white rice in separated grains that don't stick together usually prefer the texture of long grain brown rice. Cook all types of brown rice the same, although the length of time varies, usually between 45 and 65 minutes.

Carrots Hawaiian

Whoever eats these will rave about them!

Amount: 4 Servings

1. Cut in half, then in lengthwise pieces in as even size pieces as possible:
   6 medium carrots (1 lb.) scrubbed

2. Place carrots in 1½ qt. microwave or glass dish and add:
   ¼ cup water
   2 Tbsp. lemon juice
   ¼ tsp. salt

3. Cover loosely and microwave on full power 7–8 minutes (per lb.), until crisp tender, turning or stirring halfway through cooking time, if needed.

4. Meanwhile blend in a small skillet:
   1 Tbsp. melted butter, unsalted
   1 Tbsp. honey

5. When carrots are done, bring honey-butter mixture just to a boil and add:
   cooked carrots
   1 cup pineapple tidbits (fresh or 8 oz. canned, drained)

6. Stir to coat carrots and pineapple; cook about 5 minutes.

7. Garnish with minced fresh parsley if desired.

Per serving of 4
   Exchanges: 0.5 fat, 0.25 bread, 0.5 fruit, 1.75 vegetable; 108 cal., 2 gm. protein (6%), 3.5 gm. fat (6%), 8 mg. cholesterol, 20 gm. carbohydrate (68%), 4 gm. dietary fiber, 174 mg. sodium

Favorite Tamale Pie

Amount: 6 Servings (9″ square pan or 2 qt. casserole)

1. Brown together in large fry pan:
     1 lb. seasoned ground turkey
     1 small onion, chopped
     1 small green pepper, chopped
     ⅛ tsp. garlic powder or ½ tsp. ready-to-use cut garlic

2. Stir in, simmer briefly, and pour into baking pan:
     2 cups tomato, spaghetti, or pasta sauce
     2 cups frozen corn
     2¼-oz. can sliced ripe olives, drained
     1½ tsp. chili powder
     ½ tsp. salt (with tomato sauce only)

3. To make cornmeal topping, blend the cornmeal into the cold water. Stir the butter, salt, and cornmeal mixture into the boiling water. Continue stirring over medium-low heat until thickened, about 2 minutes:
     1 cup cold water
     1 cup stoneground cornmeal
     1 cup boiling water
     1 Tbsp. butter
     ½ tsp. salt

4. Spread hot cornmeal mixture evenly over top of pie mixture completely to the edges.

5. Bake uncovered at 350° for 40–50 minutes or until crust is done. Cool and freeze.

Per serving (of 6): 346 cal., 24 gm. protein, 15 gm. fat (39%), 7 gm. dietary fiber

Orange Ambrosia

Amount: 2 Servings

1. Mix together and chill before serving:
   1 medium orange, peeled and cut in chunks
   1 cup pineapple chunks or ½ mango, cut in chunks
   2 Tbsp. raisins
   2 Tbsp. coconut, medium shred, unsweetened
      (toasted at 325° about 8 minutes)
   1 tsp. granulated fructose

Pineapple Sunshine Mold

The base of unsweetened orange juice and pineapple juice sweetened with honey makes a good gelatin salad. Tasty with *Yogurt-Sour Cream Blend*.

Amount: 8 to 10 Servings

1. In a saucepan or microwave dish (see step #3 below) stir gelatin into orange juice to soften; let stand about 5 minutes:
   ¾ cup orange juice (fresh or reconstituted frozen)
   1½ pkgs. unflavored gelatin (1 Tbsp.)

2. Meanwhile, mix together in mixing bowl:

8-oz. can crushed pineapple, unsweetened
(undrained)
6-oz. can pineapple juice, unsweetened (¾ cup)
1 orange, peeled, chopped
1 banana, sliced
¼ cup chopped pecans or sliced almonds (optional)

3. To dissolve gelatin, place softened gelatin in microwave on full power for 1½ to 2 minutes, or heat to full boil in small pan on range top, stirring constantly.

4. Blend honey into dissolved gelatin and combine with remaining ingredients in mixing bowl:
   3 Tbsp. honey

5. Pour into 8″ or 9″ square pan; chill in refrigerator until set.

6. To serve: Cut into squares for individual servings. Place on individual salad plates or serving platter on lettuce greens. Garnish, as desired with mint leaves, strawberry halves.

Per serving of 8 (nuts and garnish not included)
  Exchanges: 0.5 bread, 1.5 fruit; 90 cal., 2 gm. protein (8%), 22 gm. carbohydrate (92%), 1 gm. dietary fiber, 2 mg. sodium

1½ tsp. pecans per serving add: 0.5 Fat Exchange, 25 calories, 2.5 gm. fat

Variations:

1. Add ½ cup seedless grapes, cut in half.

2. Omit banana and orange; add ¾ cup chopped celery and ¾ cup grated carrot.

Per serving of 8 (garnish not included)
  Exchanges: 0.25 bread, 1 fruit, 0.25 vegetable; 76 cal., 2 gm. protein (9%), 18 gm. carbohydrate (91%), 1 gm. dietary fiber, 18 mg. sodium

3. Mold and serve in attractive glass bowl, or mold individual servings in custard cups to unmold and serve in lettuce cups.

Note: Use only canned pineapple in gelatin salads. Fresh pineapple contains an enzyme that interferes with gelling. It is destroyed by cooking.

Tuna Noodle Yummy

A variation of Fettucini. Utilizing the microwave simplifies and speeds preparation of this tasty casserole, but it may also be prepared on range top.

Amount: 6 Servings

1. Bring water to a boil, add ingredients and continue boiling until noodles are tender, 5 to 6 minutes:
   4 quarts water
   ¼ tsp. salt
   1 tsp. olive oil
   8 oz. whole grain noodles

2. Drain and rinse noodles quickly, cooling them as little as possible.

3. Meanwhile, combine in microwave dish, cover, and microwave on full power 2 to 3 minutes (or sauté on range top until just tender):
   ½ onion, chopped
   ½ cup or large rib celery, chopped
   1 to 3 Tbsp. water

4. Combine in glass casserole or microwave dish:
   cooked celery and onion, drained
   1 cup nonfat plain yogurt
   ½ cup light sour cream (as Knudsen Nice n' Light)
   ⅓ to ½ cup Parmesan cheese

2 Tbsp. flour (whole wheat pastry preferred)
6.5-oz. can water pack tuna (50% less salt preferred)
½ tsp. salt
½ cup frozen green peas
cooked noodles (fold in gently)

5. Cover and heat in microwave until hot through, but do not allow liquid to boil.

Per serving of 6
   Exchanges: 1 meat, 0.25 milk, 0.74 fat, 2 bread, 0.25 vegetable; 260 cal., 19 gm. protein (30%), 5 gm. fat (18%), 30 mg. cholesterol, 35 gm. carbohydrate (52%), 8.5 gm. dietary fiber, 433 mg. sodium

Variation: For gourmet version, sauté the onion and celery with ¼ cup slivered or sliced almonds in ¼ cup butter, unsalted; increase to ½ cup Parmesan cheese.

Per serving of 6
   Exchanges: 1.25 meat, 0.25 milk, 3 fat, 2 bread, 0.25 vegetable; 373 cal., 21 gm. protein (23%), 16.5 gm. fat (40%), 52 mg. cholesterol, 36 gm. carbohydrate, 9 gm. dietary fiber, 487 mg. sodium

9 | Things Happen When Women Care About Hospitality

———————— ♥ ————————

Cheerfully share your home with those
who need a meal or a place to stay for the
night (1 Peter 4:9 TLB).

*H*OSPITALITY IS CARING. We can entertain all we
like, but not until we care does it become hospitality. It doesn't take much—just the heart to care for your
guests. My mother, at 77, lived in a one-room efficiency
apartment on the fifteenth floor of a senior citizen building. She continually shared hospitality with a cup of tea or
coffee, a few raisins and mixed nuts, perhaps some banana
bread or cookies. Her guests always felt special, sipping
tea in real china cups with a flower or rose in a drinking
glass and many times a candle on the table. These simple
touches say, "Welcome, I care."

Many times we feel things have to be perfect: the right
time, the right house, the right food. But who says what is
right? All it takes is the warm, caring attitude of a loving
heart.

We have some affluent, fancy friends who have everything, so to speak, that is right. Silver, china and crystal,
candelabras, and matching cloths and napkins that go just
perfectly with the china and crystal. To entertain them is
intimidating, to say the least. My thought is, "Why am I
having them over?" To reciprocate, I guess. I can't possibly
meet their level of perfection. In my heart I care and love

217

these friends, but my "self" says, "I can't do it." I was visiting on the phone one day with Georgia and, before I could catch myself, I invited them over for dinner—tonight, I said, "and I hope you don't mind soup and salad." It was a chilly California January day, and I'd put on a pot of home-made chicken vegetable soup. I must say I got excited about being able to have fellowship with such special people. Bob built a fire in the living room fireplace; I threw a checkered cloth over the coffee table, picked what flowers I could find, lit two candles, and served my famous tossed green salad, chicken soup, and crusty bread. We were all on diets, so for dessert we had sliced fruit with a Tbsp. of granola on top. Here's Georgia's thank-you note:

> Dear Bob and Em,
>
> I don't know when Jim and I have had a greater evening. It truly was an evening from soup to nuts. The food and sitting on the floor by the fire was a fun change. In fact, Jim wants me to do the same thing next time we have friends over. Thank you for the great idea and a memorable evening.
> Love, Georgia

I later heard from mutual friends what a great evening Jim and Georgia had in our home, eating delicious soup.

Some people use the excuse of not having enough room—too small a house or apartment. My mother only had a one-room efficiency apartment and she shared hospitality. It reminds me of the two years we lived in a very small condo when our children were in high school. Brad played varsity football, and Jenny was a cheerleader. It was the beginning of football season and the players had worked hard in practice to prepare for the year. We wanted to get acquainted with these young people since our children would be involved with them. Bob and I suggested we have a tostada feed for all 50 football players and cheerleaders after their first game. Our kids thought it was a neat idea.

We called it a Mexican Mountain Fiesta. Bob and I genuinely cared about these young people.

Jenny and Brad were thrilled and excited to have them all over; however, we had several negatives. Our condo complex had little guest parking. Fifty people could not fit into our 1300-square-foot condo—especially 200-plus-pound players and jumpy, giddy, cute cheerleaders. We had a lot of reasons to say, "Forget the whole idea." Here's what we did. The school bus dropped all the players off at our front door. We converted our two-car garage into a serve-yourself food buffet, set up long tables for the food, and decorated the walls with sheets of butcher paper, pom-poms, and construction-paper footballs. We had each person sign the paper with their names and cute sayings. Many wrote a big "Thank-you! Great fun! Let's do it again next year."

I served big bowls of tortilla chips, refried beans, chopped tomatoes, green onions, chopped olives, lettuce, ground beef, cheese, salsa, and anything else you can think of. They grabbed a paper plate and built the biggest mountains I've ever seen to this day.

That evening those young people sang school songs and stayed on and on. Bob and I sat in our little family room as students came in and out to visit with us. It was a great way to get to know the young people our children were going to spend much time with. One young football player named Scott came in, sat on the floor, and for almost one hour didn't stop talking. He told us things we didn't even want to know. We just listened. When Scott got up to leave, he shook Bob's hand and said, "Mr. Barnes, this has been a super evening, and I don't know when I enjoyed talking to someone as much as I have you." We laughed later because Bob hadn't said more than 20 words to Scott in over an hour. Look what we would have missed if we used the excuse that our home was too small. I've found over the years we can do whatever we *care* to do. Many of those students we still know, and they continue to remind us of the Mexican Mountain Fiesta.

Last year Bob and I had the opportunity to do a seminar for Bob and Nan Simonsen, a Christian couple who happen to own one of the fastest-growing Tupperware dealerships in the United States. They are eager to teach their people ways of saving time to give more hours to their distributors so they can have time for home, family, and their Tupperware businesses. Nan is a very attractive, dark-haired, bubbly dynamo. She has a love for the Lord, her family, and her Tupperware people. I was really drawn to Nan and thought, "Here's a gal I'd love to get to know better." After the seminar, Bob and Nan gave us a tour of their operation and we discovered we attended the same church (we have a very large church). We had expressed our feelings of wanting to spend time to get to know them and fellowship when Nan said, "How about brunch after church Sunday?" We happened to be in town and accepted the invitation. You could not find a harder-working, busier couple than the Simonsens. When we arrived on Sunday, she had a super waffle bar ready—all *Eating Right* foods. Just our cup of tea. What she had done was *cared* enough to read our book *Eating Right* (well, most of the book) and served us what she knew we would love. It was their first waffle bar brunch, and even their 13-year-old son, Erik, and his friend enjoyed it.

I was very impressed with the care Nan took and the time she gave to share hospitality with others. As I sat at their food bar and watched her, I was super-impressed with her kitchen organization. Her pantry was chock-full from vitamins to Jello, all in beautiful Tupperware sealed tight and sound.

Guess what I did the next week? I ordered Tupperware and had one of her distributors Tupperize our pantry. It's been a year now, and I'm still excited about my organized pantry and the Simonsens.

Here's Nan's Waffle Bar Brunch as found in our *Holiday Menu Recipe Book* (see page 6 for ordering information).

——————— ♥ ———————

Holiday Waffle Bar

Emilie has served this delightful buffet for her Ladies' Christmas Tea with great success! Or serve it as an Easter brunch. Great anytime of year for any occasion and for any meal!

Orange Juice
Four Grain Waffles
Fresh Strawberries or *Strawberry Topping*
Whipped Cream
Mixed Fruit Bowl
Whipped Butter   Maple Syrup
Frozen Vanilla and/or Vanilla Yogurt
Nuts 'n Coconut
Turkey Sausage, optional

Orange Juice

If you have access to an economical supply of fresh oranges, quick work of juicing them can be made with an electric juice squeezer. Plan on the following:

5 lbs. oranges per 6 servings (approx. 8 oz. each). One 4.5 oz. medium orange yields about 1/3 cup juice.

If juice is squeezed in advance, cover tightly and store in dark in refrigerator to minimize vitamin C loss.

To prepare frozen orange juice concentrate, plan on the following amount:

One 12-oz. can orange juice concentrate per 6
servings. One 12-oz. can yields 48 oz. (six 8-oz.
glasses).

Four Grain Waffles

Absolutely delicious—and no wheat! This waffle party recipe has been used time and again with many groups. Good
served anytime of year for any meal for family or for guests.
A waffle feed is a "no-fail fun feed!" The batter makes
pancakes, too.

Amount: 3 to 4 waffles (serves 6)

1. Blend together in mixing bowl:
      1 cup brown rice flour (see note after directions)
      1 cup oat flour
      ½ cup millet flour
      ½ cup toasted buckwheat flour or buckwheat flour
      1 Tbsp. baking powder (low sodium baking powder
          from health food store preferred)
      1 tsp. salt

2. Separate eggs, being very careful not to get any egg yolk
   into the egg whites (fat ir the yolk prevents whites from
   whipping up):
      4 eggs

3. Blend into the dry ingredients:
      1½ to 2 cups buttermilk (as desired for consistency)
      ¼ cup oil (light olive or canola oil from health food
          store preferred) or melted butter
      4 egg yolks

4. Whip the egg whites at high speed with electric mixer
   until stiff enough to hold peaks, but not dry.

5. Gently fold egg whites into waffle batter. It is not necessary to blend in the whites until they disappear. The less
   mixing, the lighter the waffles will be.

6. Spray hot waffle iron once with no-stick cooking spray (Olive Oil Pam preferred), before making the first waffle. Scoop batter to center of waffle iron with a measuring cup.

Variations:

1. Add to batter: 1 cup fresh or frozen blueberries.

2. Add to batter: 1/2 cup sunflower seeds or chopped nuts.

3. Omit egg yolks for lower fat and cholesterol content.

4. Omit oil or butter; waffles will not be as crisp.

5. Use sour milk, or yogurt thinned to buttermilk consistency in place of buttermilk.

---

* A variety of whole grain flours are usually available in health food stores. We usually mill our flours from the whole grains, using 2/3 cup brown rice, 2/3 cup whole oats (rolled oats can be milled if whole oats aren't available), 1/3 cup whole millet, 1/3 cup toasted buckwheat (kasha) or sprouting buckwheat (darker, stronger flavor, and much less expensive).

Strawberry Topping

Serve over Four Grain Waffles, Angel Food Cake, Honey Cheesecake, or Yogurt Pie. We make this topping if the berries are slightly overripe, or with frozen berries when fresh strawberries are not in season. This recipe works well with any other fresh or frozen berries.

Amount: 1 1/2 to 2 cups (serves 4 to 6)

1. Blend together with a wire whisk in a saucepan:
   about 1/2 cup fresh or frozen strawberries, crushed
   about 1/2 cup cold water (room temperature okay)
   2 Tbsp. cornstarch or arrowroot powder (health food store)
   1 to 2 Tbsp. honey or crystalline fructose (health food store)

2. Cook over medium heat, stirring constantly, until thickened and clear.

3. Stir in and heat through:

    1½ cups fresh or frozen strawberries, quartered

4. Adjust sweetening to taste with more honey or fructose as desired.

Whipped Cream

Amount: 2 cups (Serves 6, ⅓ cup each)

1. In electric mixer on high speed whip for about 30 seconds:

    ½ pint whipping or heavy cream

2. Add gradually, continuing to whip until thickened:

    2 Tbsp. mild-flavored honey or crystalline fructose (health food store)

Mixed Fruit Bowl

Serve a bowl of two, three, or more fresh fruits to go on top of waffles or alongside. The following are some of our favorite combinations, but only the season need be limiting. A single fresh fruit, chopped or sliced, is also delicious.

Amount: Allow ½ cup per serving

    strawberries, peaches, blueberries
    peaches, pineapple
    nectarines, pineapple
    nectarines, blueberries
    peaches, blackberries

If desired, sprinkle fruit lightly with crystalline fructose or sugar.

Whipped Butter

Whipped butter is 20 calories lower than butter per Tbsp., and easier to spread. It is easy to make your own with soft butter. The added air whipped into the butter will increase the volume by about one-third. Serve in an attractive small bowl or on a small round plate.

Amount: About ⅔ cup

1. Bring to room temperature until very soft, or soften in microwave on simmer for about 45 seconds:

    1 cube (½ cup) butter

2. Place butter in small deep mixing bowl and whip vigorously with a wire whisk until light and creamy.

Maple Syrup

Real or pure maple syrup comes from real maple trees! It is admittedly expensive, but a little goes a long way, especially when served with fruit topping alternatives. ¼ cup per person is more than ample, and 2 Tbsp. per serving is usually adequate. 1 pint will serve 12 to 16.

Yogurt

Yogurt is very delicious with fruit and waffles! After serving hundreds of guests this combination, we have learned that the two most enjoyed are Vanilla Yogurt and Frozen Vanilla Yogurt. Sometimes we serve both, sometimes one or the other. Guests generally eat more Frozen Yogurt than Vanilla Yogurt. Plan on the following amounts:

    Frozen Vanilla Yogurt: 8 servings per quart (½ cup each)
    Vanilla Yogurt: 16 servings per quart (¼ cup each)

We recommend lowfat or nonfat yogurt made with active bacteria culture and containing either honey or fructose.

Nuts 'n Coconut

A bowl each of nuts and coconut are a fun addition to the waffle bar buffet table. Purchase unroasted, unsalted nuts, and unsweetened coconut. The health food store will have these if not available in the supermarket. Plan on having on hand the following amounts:

nuts: 12 to 24 servings per ½ lb. (1 to 2 Tbsp. each)
such as pecans, walnuts, sliced almonds
coconut: 12 to 24 servings per ¼ lb. (1 to 2 Tbsp. each)

Turkey Sausage

A great and tasty alternative to bacon and pork sausage, ground turkey contains ¼ the fat of pork sausage and less than half the calories, and ⅕ the fat of bacon with less than ⅓ the calories. Many guests cannot believe they are eating turkey when they are served this recipe!

Amount: 12 patties (Serves 6)

1. Mix together thoroughly with a fork:
   1 lb. ground turkey
   1 tsp. salt
   ½ tsp. nutmeg
   ½ tsp. sage
   ½ tsp. thyme
   ⅛ tsp. cayenne pepper

2. Shape into 12 small patties. Fry in ungreased skillet or bake at 350° for 10 to 15 minutes in a shallow pan until done. Do not overcook or patties will become tough. Oven baking produces juicier patties and is easier when feeding a crowd.

———— ♥ ————

I asked Nan to share some hospitality ideas with me for this book and here is what she wrote:

We are so busy in our lives we need to *purposely* give attention to the everyday things that can make our lives lovelier, such as keeping a vase of fresh flowers in an obvious place, or several places in the house. Planting roses or other flowers *for this purpose* makes sense.

Women need to give attention to their appearance when it seems to matter least: in the evenings at home, when the children come home in the afternoon, when running errands. It takes so little extra time to freshen our looks and put on something coordinated and nice and shows respect to those we live with and come in contact with.

Greeting guests with anticipation at the door, even casual acquaintances, is *so nice.* Seeing those guests to the door and bidding them goodbye with a hug leaves such a nice feeling for both parties. I'm not talking about "best behavior" for special occasions. I'm talking about reviving and using basic good manners and grace in our everyday lives with our everyday acquaintances.

—Nan Simonsen
Riverside, California

It's no wonder their Tupperware business is a success.

A Special Christmas Friendship Tea

Every year I have a Christmas tea for all my lady friends. The past five years I've served my famous waffle bar. It's a hit every year, but more than food and Christmas these women leave with hearts filled with love, knowing I care for them and our friendship. I wouldn't have to do this. It's a lot of time and work, from preparing the house early for Christmas, cooking the food, and sweeping the walkways to lighting the candles and oil lamps. Bob builds the fire, puts on the music, and sets the serving table with a centerpiece of fresh pine greens, poinsettia, and pine cones. I have great solid-red plates I bought at my favorite discount store, Pic 'N Save, eight years ago for 98 cents each. These have been used and used and borrowed so often, not only do I use these for Christmas, but on Valentine's Day, Fourth of July, and any other time I use a red theme.

It's a lot of work—not to even mention the clean-up and put-away effort. By December, we are pretty exhausted. Our holiday seminars begin in October and end around December 10. Most years we've completed 32 seminars in about 45 days. So to give a Christmas Tea and family entertaining exhausts me to just think about it. But we do it. Worth it? You bet! Last year at my tea, after the waffle bar was demolished, we sat around the fire. I gave each lady a small candle. As I lit mine, I then lit with my candle, the candle of the person sitting next to me and shared a Christmas blessing. "Thank you for your loving friendship, your prayers for us. May God bless you and your family with a warm and memorable Christmas." As each one lit the next person's candle and shared, I knew then why it was so worthwhile to give and care for these ladies. By the time all our candles were lit, we all had teary eyes, wet cheeks, and mascara running down our faces. It was truly tissue time. Oh, how good it felt! Bob always teases me by saying you'll know when Emilie's tea is a success if the women leave in tears. Bob also enjoys these times of hospitality and using our home to glorify our Lord. After the holidays, birthdays, and many years of giving and caring, Bob presented me with a certificate (see p. 229). It touched my heart to realize Bob cared and appreciated the extra miles it takes to give hospitality.

In the summer of '89 we did a seminar in Bishop, a small town in central California. Our long-time dear friends, Dan and Linda Densmoor, hosted us. They went to Bishop to build and open a Taco Bell fast-food store. Most people would rather die than to think of having us in their home for three days. Just the thought of cleaning, organizing, and food planning quickly keeps families from volunteering

Certificate of Appreciation

This Certifies That

Emilie Barnes

has given outstanding service
and is hereby recognized for excellence in

Homemaking

This Certificate is awarded by

Bob Barnes

on this ___29th___ day of ___June___ 19 _89_ ___Bob Barnes___ to house us. Linda and Dan are cool—they charge right through and also know we don't care if they want to *care* for us. We really are easy to please.

I was totally impressed. Upon our arrival, the table was set for dinner. After dinner, Linda set the table for breakfast. After breakfast, she set the table for dinner again. Linda is blessed. When Dan's mother died, she left Linda with lovely dishes so Linda has several sets and she uses them all. We all helped in the cleanup. Dan does all the ironing (and has for years), so you can see they have defined certain jobs for each other over their married years and raising four children. I say all that to point out that Linda does have the gift of hospitality. She works with such ease, and yet things are not perfect but perfectly comfortable. Those few days together were wonderful. Here are a few ideas Linda shared with me of ways she *cares* through hospitality.

Gift Wrap Party

Have friends (6 to 12) over for an evening of Christmas gift wrapping. They bring the gifts they need to wrap, paper, tags, ribbon, tape, and anything else they might want to use. Everyone wraps gifts together, and begs and borrows from each other. Linda then serves cookies and/or snacks. A fun evening and your wrapping stress is over. Plus, this will help you to get Christmas shopping done by the wrapping party date.

One year Linda and her daughter drove to San Francisco (a two-hour drive from Bishop), rented a hotel room, shopped for Christmas presents all day, had a lovely dinner out, purchased gift wrap, and spent the next day in the hotel wrapping all their gifts. They drove home and were done, plus it was a great time of mother/daughter *caring*.

Wood, Hay, and Stubble Party

For this impromptu party, call several friends and say, "Come over Friday evening and bring whatever you have left over in the freezer or refrigerator." It's fun, and many crazy combinations have been eaten.

This is also fun after Christmas. Put on a pot of tea or coffee and have friends bring leftover Christmas fruitcake, cookies, turkey, gravy, mash potatoes, cranberry sauce, punch, etc.

———————— ♥ ————————

One woman wrote,

By the time the Christmas season arrived, I was exhausted, frustrated, and depressed because of the thought of spending money. I felt my family would surely understand if we just skipped Christmas altogether. My husband had been working 70 hours a week. He, too, was tired, but to skip Christmas was to him the greatest discouragement of all! I couldn't disappoint him and our 15-year-old son, our daughter, her husband, and our baby grandson's first Christmas. So this is what I did.

I had hired my 13-year-old cousin during that winter vacation to help me move some things in from the rubble in the garage. She asked if her two younger cousins could help. I agreed. I witnessed their excitement at bringing in some of those things I'd tucked away, like the oven mitts with the spatulas, wire whisks, and wooden spoons and the Bible covers, the tins with the muffin recipes attached, the baskets to put food in and so on. I asked them to help me wrap (we used the gift bags and instant bows). Their enthusiasm was just what I needed to make it, and since I had taken the counsel in your book *The Complete Holiday Organizer* (Harvest House Publishers) and had invested a little here and there, everything came together with a little effort. I photocopied a drawing I had done for our Christmas letter, the girls addressed and stamped the letters and got them out in the mail for Christmas. I was pleasantly surprised at how much my earlier investments in the gifts had saved me both in time and money.

Finally we went to the grocery store for eggnog, sparkling cider, and a turkey and all the trimmings. We stopped by our friend's Christmas tree farm and picked out a lonely but beautiful tree and watched him chop it down and load it into the car. The rest is a memory of a holiday that was complete in every way: good smells, pleasant tastes, and sharing.

Emilie, your ideas have given me direction and I am glad and thankful I responded and did my part. "And ye shall rejoice in all that ye put your hand unto, ye and your households, wherein the Lord thy God hath blessed thee" (Deuteronomy 12:7).

—Chris
Hemet, California

Iowa Ladies Care

Chris seemed pushed and overwhelmed, but she *cared*. However, once she got started and organized her holiday, it all fell together beautifully and she received a blessing.

In September I found myself in the small, friendly town of Mt. Pleasant, Iowa. I was totally surprised and overwhelmed when this small Iowa town attracted over 150 women to the "More Hours in My Day" seminar.

When Betty Scott booked the seminar with my Bob, she said, "We're stepping out on faith that we'll fill our church with women that Emilie can help and teach."

I know that committee prayed, and eight months later God blessed those ladies and answered their prayer as those women arrived that Saturday morning. But that is not the end of the story.

These women wanted me to see their part of the country and experience their way of life. I was elated! Six Iowa ladies took me on an incredible tour for a California city girl. Our tour guide was an 84-year-young retired schoolteacher who was called "Teach" most of her life. The home she lived in was the home she grew up in. She never married but *cared* for students, teaching high school physical education for over 60 years. "Teach" took us to little towns, antique shops, and cornfields. We ended up—would you believe—in the home of an Amish woman who shared her hospitality with all of us. The simple farmhouse was set on 30 acres of cornfields—no electricity, no car, but a great horse and buggy. The floors in the farmhouse were raw wood floors, not carpeted; the furniture very simple; there was no TV, no radio, no electric lamps—only oil, no automatic stove, washer, dryer, refrigerator, microwave, mixer, blender, food processor, or any other appliance. Yet this woman single-handedly expressed her love and warmth and caring spirit as she served all seven of us an incredible luncheon.

The table was simply set with a plastic tablecloth, paper napkins (no centerpiece), and dishes I'm sure were handed down at least four generations. Here is what we ate and we ate the whole thing: fried chicken. She fried it first, then baked it. Moist and tender (you bet!), plus she raises the chickens and prepared this one early that day. Corn on the cob grown on their farm, real mashed potatoes (not from a box), cole slaw, fresh-baked hot bread and churned butter with homemade jam, chicken dressing and gravy, homemade noodles, tapioca pudding, date pudding (this was my favorite—it was like a truffle with whipped cream, nuts, and dates), and vanilla pudding. Guess what? That wasn't all. We had dessert yet to come. She single-handedly served, cleared, and cooked it all. She insisted we not help; it was her joy. Out came two beautiful, fresh peach pies with a lattice top sprinkled with sugar and topped off with homemade ice cream, hot tea, coffee, or iced tea. This adorable woman then sat with us, visited, and gave us the opportunity to ask her questions about her family, the Amish lifestyle and Amish beliefs. I know she loved us as much as we loved her. We rolled out that day. My only regret was that my Bob wasn't there to enjoy this priceless experience that I'll never forget.

To top off the day, "Teach" brought us back to her 100-year-old Victorian home for a tour of the five bedrooms, quilts and pillows she made, and heirloom furniture.

My memory of Iowa didn't stop there. A dear lady in our group—Lois Martin—sent me (for our harvest table) dried Indian corn, beans, gourds, and other special Iowa memories plus a lovely picture of the Amish horse and buggy. Thank-you, Iowa, for *caring* for one of your servants. Believe me, they taught me far more than I gave them. How often this happens when I leave a church. I receive far more than I give. And that's the rest of the story.

Lasagna and Cheesecake Hospitality

Five years ago we started a tradition with our son Brad's college friends. Now we didn't intend it to become a tradition, but that's what happened and we're thrilled. Brad came to us and asked if we would host his friends in our California country home. We live in a 45-year-old home that is a converted barn (well, a bit nicer than that), set on an acre of property in the middle of the city of Riverside. This time the 50 young adults who arrived had a bit more room than the 1300-square-foot condo that we fed the football players in. We were pleased to see that Brad had a *caring* heart for his college friends and wanted to share hospitality with them. The menu was Brad's choice: Mom's famous lasagna, green salad, crusty garlic bread and creamy cheesecake. I'm proud to say Brad didn't dump the preparation on Bob and me. Brad's great in the kitchen and has a real touch with food, so we worked together to present this meal to his (and now our) friends.

The evening was a big success. We met girlfriends and singles, and fell in love with these young adults who had strong goals to achieve after college. We were amazed at the thank-you notes we received. We'd created an evening of modeling and memories.

We've repeated this same evening for over five years now—same menu. They insist we serve Emilie's lasagna and cheesecake. Many of these men are bringing their fiancées to meet us. It's like they can't get married without our blessings. We've attended some great weddings. This past year we felt we would skip the party due to the fact Brad would not be available since he took an assignment for one year in Boston. The group wouldn't see it. "So what if Brad's not there—it's tradition!" Now they *care* to share with us and one another. Brad will be back in California this spring, and the first thing he'll plan is the traditional lasagna party. It goes to show that hospitality doesn't even have to be in your own home. Here are the lasagna and cheesecake recipes:

Emilie's Best Lasagna

"Best lasagna in the whole world!" Emilie serves this every Christmas holiday to 60 young adults with a big green salad topped with her Olive Oil-Vinegar Dressing and red cherry tomatoes. It is always a party hit. No need to precook the lasagna noodles for this recipe!

Amount: Serves 6 to 8 (One 9″ x 13″ pan)

Oven: 350°   Bake 1 hour, uncovered

1. Brown:
   > 1 lb. Italian sausage, skinned or Italian turkey sausage (such as Louis Rich brand, supermarket meat department or ask butcher)
   > 2 cloves garlic, crushed

2. Stir in and simmer while preparing remaining ingredients:
   > 1 Tbsp. sweet basil leaves (if possible use fresh)
   > 1 large can tomato puree (28 or 29 oz.)
   > 6-oz. can tomato paste

3. Meanwhile, mix together:

2 eggs, beaten
3 cups fresh ricotta cheese
½ cup grated Parmesan cheese
2 Tbsp. parsley flakes
1 Tbsp. salt
½ tsp. pepper

4. Thinly slice:
   1 lb. mozzarella cheese

5. Spread ¼ cup sauce evenly over bottom of 9″ x 13′ baking pan or Pyrex dish.

6. Make about 3 layers of ingredients in order given:
   1 box raw, uncooked lasagna noodles (whole grain from health food store preferred or spinach pasta)
   Ricotta cheese mixture
   Sauce
   Mozzarella cheese

7. Bake uncovered at 350° for 1 hour until noodles are tender.

Emilie's Cheesecake

Crust:

1 pkg. graham crackers
1 stick butter
1 pkg. walnuts or pecans

Put nuts in processor with blade in and chop. Put on grater blade and grate graham crackers and keep mixing until evenly blended.

Filling:

4 eggs
1 cup sugar
Juice of ½ lemon
2 tsp. vanilla

Mix in food processor. Put on grater blade and put four 8-oz. packages cream cheese through (one at a time) and mix until blended. Put in a pan (spring-type is best—9" or 10") and cook at 350° for 50 minutes.

Topping:

2 cups sour cream
1 tsp. vanilla
¼ cup sugar

After the cheesecake cools (5–10 minutes) put topping on and cook another 10 minutes. Make at least one day ahead. Optional: Top with strawberries, blueberries, or cherries. Too many calories to list, but worth it.

Christine's Tea Party

Hospitality is important to teach to our children. For them to experience, feel, and be a part of the event will not only create a memory but give them tools to work with in the future.

I adore our 7-year-old granddaughter, Christine. She is the cutest, sweetest little person God has put into our lives. Last summer I invited her and one of her girlfriends, Leah, to come over for a tea party. When their moms dropped them off, I had them put on an apron and into the kitchen we went to bake cookies for their party. We had a great time visiting as we measured and dumped the ingredients into the mixing bowl.

Next we planned where the party was to be held. They chose our front-lawn area by our fish and duck pond with the large waterfall. It was a perfect choice for a warm summer day with lots of surrounding trees to shade the area. We carried out boxes to use as a table and two little chairs I had that fit their cute little frames perfectly.

Next came a cloth for the table and real china cups and saucers. I have a 35-year-old cup and saucer collection.

Many of the cups were passed down from my mother. Yes, these are special and yes, it was a chance to take, but it would be worth it to teach the girls about pretty, special table settings. As I watched them choose which cup and saucer they wanted to put out for tea, they chatted about how careful they needed to be. It made them feel very special and grown up as they carried the tray out to their tea table.

Next came flowers for the table. With scissors in hand, they picked a small bouquet of fresh daisies. This is something Christine and I have done since she was 2 years old. She knows to pick longer stems and even how to arrange them in a vase. Place them in easily and never force the stem where it doesn't want to go.

Our table was complete and looked oh, so pretty. The cookies were out of the oven and cold milk was chosen instead of tea—and that's okay for a tea party. After all, the English always put milk in their teacups. So cold milk went into the teapot and was refrigerated until we got dressed.

Out came the dress-up box, and the girls had a ball dressing up for the ladies' tea with old lace curtains for skirts and shawls. Hats and gloves, purses, and high heels completed their outfits. Teatime was here and those two little first-grade girls had a lovely time eating cookies and drinking "English tea." They sat at the tea table for a lot longer than I thought they would. The whole process took about three hours. A memory—you bet (at least for Grammie it was).

The cleaning team came in next, so off came the dress-up clothes and on went the aprons again. All was fine, with no damage or breakage. I'm glad I did it. Teaching hospitality to 7-year-olds has benefits that will continue long after I'm gone and will hopefully be passed on by them one day to a couple of cuties like them.

I've discovered that hospitality can take time. Not too many people are more involved and busier than we are. But the priority of *caring* for others through hospitality touches the heart and opens the spirit to one day talk and share the *caring* and love that God gave us through sending the ultimate *caring* love gift, His Son Jesus Christ, Messiah, Lord of lords, King of kings, God Almighty, Savior.

Reach out and *care* for someone who needs the touch of hospitality. The time you spend caring today will be a love gift that will blossom into the fresh joy of God's Spirit in the future.

> When God's children are in need, you be the one to help them out. And get into the habit of inviting guests home for dinner or, if they need lodging, for the night (Romans 12:13 TLB).

——————— ♥ ———————

Let the "angel unaware"
be in your home.

10 | Caring Through Friendships

———— ♥ ————

The more you love the more you'll find that life is good and friends are kind... and only what we give away enriches us from day to day.[1]

—Helen Steiner Rice

IF SOMEONE WERE TO ask me, "Who is your best friend?" without much thought I would say my Bob. I can tell Bob many hurts and ask his advice. He listens and usually doesn't give advice until I ask. He is my sounding board, and his wisdom is beyond mine. I'm very fortunate. Many women don't feel that way or perhaps don't have husbands. Even though I receive all of that strength from Bob, I have a need and desire for close friendships. I have many friends whose friendships have developed over 25 years. We have cared, cried, prayed, laughed, and loved together. My Newport Beach friend, Yoli Brogger, has been a confidante. She is able to read me when I couldn't read myself. She has done my *hair* (she is a professional hair stylist), has assisted in decorating several of our *homes* (she's also a talented interior designer), and has healed my *heart* over the years. She has given to me when I didn't give to her and never ever complained or asked why I hadn't called or why she hadn't been invited over. Because of friends, our families have been enriched. Our husbands have become friends, their children and our children have become friends, and we've met friends of friends of friends... it could go on and on.

When Betty Scott of Iowa lost a portion of her middle finger, her friend Lois gathered ladies to come and clean Betty's home for her. Betty says, "I had mixed emotions, but I knew scripturally that I needed to humble myself. God blessed through that in many ways because I needed to be served and observe that there are folks who do something without expecting anything in return." Since then Betty and Lois have developed a true gift of help and have organized a women's ministry service in their church called Harmony Helpers. Here are some of the friendship ways of caring these women are presently using:

———————— ♥ ————————

1. *Birthdays*—One of our artistic ladies created 12 different postcard greetings and sends them out to the women who are directly involved in the ministry.

2. *Decorating*—This lady is in charge of working with our minister of music who is in charge of worship. The goal is to decorate in a manner that draws us closer to our Creator by enhancing the worship service.

3. *Encouragement*—This lady is very creative and uses her poetry and sense of humor to show us in a practical way that "a merry heart doeth good like medicine" (that is a vital need today for our busy ladies).

4. *Fellowship*—One lady is informed about our church potlucks, fellowships, etc. and calls another lady who represents those who are responsible for organizing for that particular month. Each of the areas that represent our church take responsibility for all functions during a designated month and one lady is in charge of each area.

5. *Food pantry*—Available to needy families, stocked by our ladies.

6. *Funerals*—Like the fellowships, we've divided the responsibilities into areas with one lady in charge who calls another who is in the area of the deceased person. We provide whatever the family desires (i.e., home-cooked meals at church, or at their homes).

7. *Gift boxes*—Every year we send approximately 90 boxes of treats (homecooked candies, cookies—each individually wrapped in foil. Also boxes of raisins, nuts, popcorn, etc.) to servicemen, college students, shut-ins, etc. Each box contains a greeting and some of our pamphlets to encourage. We've begun to do this in October because college students have been away long enough to get homesick and it isn't too close to Thanksgiving. This is well-received, naturally!

8. *Missionaries*—We have practical things at church such as Tupperware that they may take with them back to the field.

9. *Evangelism*—Tract ministry.

10. *Seniors*—We interview seniors with a tape recorder to get their views on important issues. We then publish these ideas in our newsletter. Also, our older generation (80+) have given their testimonies in our worship service.

11. *Babysitting*—One of our ladies had an operation and has two children, so another lady took a sign-up sheet to church with the times and days that women were needed to go to the mother's home and be with the children (keeping in mind, of course, that Mom could not lift her little ones). Also, a sheet for meals was organized. The recovering patient reported that she did not know it could be so much fun recovering from surgery. And all this took place at Christmastime!

12. *Moving expenses*—One couple moved from our church family but couldn't afford to paint their home, so a crew of volunteers (including several teens) gathered at their home on a Saturday and finished the painting that day. Food was provided as well as all equipment. The couple hardly recognized their home.

13. *There are many opportunities to help ladies clean their homes* such as when they come home from having a baby or they have been ill for extended periods of time or some big event comes up and they simply don't have time to prepare. The mother of the wife of one of our ministers was diagnosed with cancer two weeks before her daughter was going to be married. Many, many opportunities were there and many people responded. There were lots of tears of anguish and joy. Praise Him! The mother's cancer is in complete remission now!

14. *Flock groups* in each community representing our assembly have done things such as send around a message on the telephone chain to ask for enough money for a new washer and dryer for our pastor (with five little ones, it was needed). They've gone to widows' homes to rake leaves and meet plumbing and electrical needs. Also they will go and say, "I'm here to work (tools in hand). What can I do?" (They precede this by a phone call for everyone's convenience.)

15. *One heartwarming story*—One of our dear couples in their 70's was told by their family of five children that they were all going to converge on their country home and build a double-car garage with breezeway. In addition, the children painted their parents' home. The families planned their vacations around this gala event and accomplished their mission (in spite of the fact that they have well water and ran out of water running the paint remover. They had to trek to one of their homes close by and haul water in to finish the job). These folks persevere and are a wonderful privilege to know.

All this happened because a woman cared about her dear friend and then moved a team in to clean her home. Many lives have been ministered to in the name of friendship.

Keri from Downey, California, had a friend that knew she was going through some hard times. The friend began sending Keri uplifting cards in the mail every other day. Keri says it was more caring in friendship than she'd ever had in life. It motivated her to try out her friend's church and soon her husband, her sister, and Keri became Christians. It was *wonderful*.

Brenda in Yucaipa, California, tells of her best friend who gave her a "coping-with-children basket of friendship." It included bath salts, a votive candle, a candy bar, a Christian romance novel, a babysitter gift certificate, aspirins, earplugs, and a bouquet of flowers. It was a great idea and so useful!

Ecclesiastes 3:1 says, "There is an appointed time for everything. And there is a time for every event under heaven."

Mary Newman in Columbus, Ohio, took this verse to heart and encourages her friends to call should they need to be cared for for a couple of hours. "Come lay on my sofa, kick your feet up, and I'll serve you tea. I'll watch your children and give you a breather before your stress becomes a crisis," Mary offered.

When I received this letter from Tania, my heart was moved by her story and the faithfulness to her friend. She writes:

I have been to your seminars and read all your books. These have inspired me to be used by God and led by His mighty power. At 18 I graduated from high school and found out I was pregnant. By November of that year I married and became a mom. The adjustment was overwhelming, so your ministry was a tremendous help. My husband was a cocaine addict, and I was date-raped, suicidal, and went through an abortion prior to our marriage. We've now been married five years and have two children.

I love to write letters to friends and I keep a list of names and the dates the letters are sent. Sometimes it gets hard when you write and write and never get a return letter. I was so discouraged after writing many letters to a high school classmate. She went away to college and became promiscuous and got into drugs. This was out of character for my Christian friend. I kept writing, wondering if my letters were doing any good or even being read. After about three years I received a phone call. She was tired of her way of life and wanted to walk seriously with Jesus and become involved with church. That was three years ago, and we're still close friends. She is now a strong Christian and engaged to a wonderful Christian man.

I've also shared the Lord with my cocaine-addicted husband. It's taken three years, but now he has grown into a wonderful Christian and leads the home as our head.

Sometimes we may tire of praying, writing, and witnessing. God knows the future and He makes all things beautiful in His time. I thank God for His faithfulness and caring about us who lead our own lives into misery only to be touched by our God who never stops writing, waiting, and loving us.

—Tania

Carrie of Sierra Madre, California, discovered the perfect solution to keeping her house clean. She had been drowning in her home of dust, dirt, and clutter. She couldn't cope. Another friend was feeling the same pressure, so together they take turns cleaning their homes. They get together every week and one week they clean one home and the following week, the other. Together they get a lot accomplished. The houses sparkle and the women have been able to share each other's company and fellowship. They feel so relaxed. Each home is thoroughly cleaned every other week, and they are able to maintain in-between. The friendship and caring that has grown between them is now more important to them than the housework that is accomplished. Yes, they were both a bit nervous at first. It's scary to admit to someone else that you are a slob and have trouble coping, but the results have been more than worth the initial risk.

Jim and Ellen Cashman of Riverside, California, have a best friend husband-and-wife relationship. Bob and I met this special couple through our church recently and are growing in love and friendship with them. Ellen gives us some part-time help as needed with our mail and shipping. This family with three children has gone through some real struggles and problems, especially financial. They stand as a testimony to what God can do if given the opportunity to grow something beautiful out of something we have spoiled.

Last year for Mother's Day Jim gave Ellen a tasting spoon he hand-carved himself. This is Jim's description of "The Tasting Spoon":

The solid stock of maple is to remind us God made us and through Jesus Christ we have been made whole and strong.

The carved design curving down the handle is to remind us that our lives here on earth will not be smooth and straight. They will have hills and detours to give us our own personal perspective and personality.

The small spoon end is to remind us that God has not given us the whole pot to swallow all at once. But through the small bites we can overcome anything through Jesus Christ, the One who strengthens us!

The finish of plain oil is to remind us the trappings of life are only a covering to cover the real person we are and the natural love and beauty God gave us all and we need to strive to see it in everyone!

As Ellen uses this spoon everyday, it reminds her of how much God has blessed them in their 20-year marriage and of how through Christ's love, anything is possible.

"Santa Claus is our friend." I read this in the editorial section of the Los Angeles *Times*, January 1990. It was written by a mother and is a great example of exhibiting friendship when you don't even know the friend.

Thanks, Santa,

This is a thank-you note to a stranger. A few weeks ago, my 3-year-old asked if he could send a letter to Santa. I found him a piece of scrap paper, and with a good deal of squirming and searching for the right word, he dictated his letter. "Dear Santa, I want a spaceship for Christmas. Love, Andrew." He decorated the letter. We addressed it to Santa at the North Pole, and put on a return address, and dropped it in the mailbox at the corner.

On December 26, we were all struggling with post-Christmas letdown, when a priority mail package came, postmarked Los Angeles, and addressed to Drew. There was no return address except for the name: Santa. Our letter was returned, along with a lovely little box of workbooks and crayons and a little note: "Dear Drew. I was all out of spaceships. I hope you like this instead. Have a very Merry Christmas. Love, Santa."

Dear Santa, I don't know where you are, but thank you a thousand times for the time and the thoughtfulness and the generosity that went into that little package. You are one of those who truly understands the spirit of Christmas, and you have made this Christmas one that my family will always remember.

—Jean Campbell
Los Angeles

During the months of October and November we book holiday seminars. These sessions include Thanksgiving and Christmas organization, gift giving and wrapping ideas, creative hospitality, building memories, establishing Christ-centered traditions, and a festival of lights. Coming from a Jewish background, I share the story of Hanukkah and then flow into the meaning of the Advent wreath and the true meaning of and reason for our Christmas season and Jesus' birthday. The women really love it and it has become a very special event for them and their family and friends. (For complete details see *The Complete Holiday Organizer*—Harvest House Publishers.)

In January I received this letter from Dorothy Segonia of Irvine, California:

> Emilie, this will bless you. In November, two years ago when you shared with us at your Christmas seminar the "I Love You because..." cards and suggested we place one under each plate at a family dinner, I thought, "What a beautiful idea." Thanksgiving came and went and Christmas came and went. I was so sure I'd be rejected that I did nothing (fear of man again). (However, remember I've been rejected by several of my family turkeys, ha, ha!) This year I prayed and God gave me the words, the verses, and the time to set apart and write 12 cards. It was magical, peaceful, loving, and reflective. The wind of the Holy Spirit moved through a room full of superficial and sarcastic talk and made it soft and sensitive.
>
> Here comes the blessing. On Josephine's card (very active aunt who lost her legs 20 years ago and never, never complains) I wrote: "I love you because you show me such courage. You give me energy and strength to go on each day when I feel down." That precious lady looked over at me and said, "I will remember this every day as I fight off this strong urge

to kill myself. Nobody has said encouraging words to me in 30 years" (tears streaming down her face). Emilie, thank you. See how God multiplies our ministry!

Josephine lives with my brother and his wife and no one has given her a reason to live. She cooks, washes, reads, needlepoints, and does fabulous caretaking at their house *with no legs*, and no one sees her as extraordinary.

Your idea and my words made her decade! Hallelujah! He alone is worthy of the praise!

I was very touched and blessed by Dorothy's willingness to be obedient to the leading of God's Spirit. It's exciting to see Dorothy—

> Standing on His promises
> Sitting in His presence
> Walking in His wisdom.

She's a great example of reaching out and touching someone's heart, of taking the risk and letting go of self despite fear of rejection. Is there someone in your life you can touch by a simple note or card to say "I Love You Because..."?

When Paula, a teacher, had a family crisis, her teacher's aide reached out and touched her life and family by caring enough to get teachers to go in together and pay for a housekeeper to come to Paula's home for three weeks and give her the relief she needed. It was a wonderful gift Paula will never forget. A friend is someone who comes in when the whole world has gone out.

I was speaking in Irving, Ohio, for a Choice Book conference and had the privilege of staying in the home of a Mennonite couple. They were moving in two days and, as I looked around, not one thing was packed or even looked like it was ready to pack. Now I was curious. I would start packing weeks and months ahead if Bob would let me. I finally asked Sandy when she would start packing to move. "Oh, no," she explained. "I don't pack at all. On moving day there will be 20-30 men here from the church. They will pack and move all the household to our new old home where the women are scrubbing, painting, and wallpapering as needed. By dinnertime, food will be brought in for everyone (all homemade), the beds will be set up and made, pictures on the walls, and children tucked in." Friends helping friends! This is the same group who told me that when a woman becomes pregnant ten ladies will show up at her house and bring sewing machines, fabric as needed, and by afternoon leave with a complete maternity wardrobe finished for the expectant mom to wear and enjoy. This absolutely overwhelms me. The support given God's children in need expresses the true meaning of friendship.

> Friendship, like the immortality of the soul, is too good to believe.
>
> —Emerson

———— ♥ ————

Be a friend to someone today.
You are loved and needed.

NOTES

Chapter 2—When Women Care For Themselves
1. Robert H. Schuller, *Self-Esteem, The New Reformation* (Waco, TX: Word Pub., 1982), pp. 17-18.
2. Adapted from Stephen R. Covey, *The Seven Habits of Highly Effective People* (New York: Simon and Schuster, 1989).
3. Jan Congo, *Free to Be God's Woman* (Ventura, CA: Regal Books, 1985), adapted from p. 94.

Chapter 3—Caring for Singles
1. Andrew Murray, source unknown.
2. "The Working Mother's Guilt," *Time* magazine, Jan. 4, 1982, p. 81.
3. Barbara G. Cashion, "Female-Headed Families: Effects on Children and Clinical Implications," *Journal of Marital and Family Therapy*, Apr. 1982, p. 77.
4. Ann Landers, "Sorry, No Medals for You, Kid," *The Press Enterprise*, Jan. 26, 1990, Sec. B-10.
5. Sherwood Eliot Wirt and Kersten Bechstrom, *Topical Encyclopedia of Living Quotations* (Minneapolis: Bethany House Publishers, 1982), p. 146.
6. Andre Bustanoby, *Being a Single Parent* (Grand Rapids, MI: The Zondervan Corp.), pp. 242-44.
7. Wirt and Bechstrom, *Topical Encyclopedia*, p. 114.

Chapter 4—Caring About Children
1. Florence Littauer, *Raising the Curtain on Raising Children* (Waco, TX: Word Books), p. 14.
2. Brenda Hunter, "The Value of Motherhood," *Focus on the Family*, 1986, pp. 9-12.
3. H. Stephen Glenn and Jane Nelsen, *Raising Self-Reliant Children in a Self-Indulgent World* (Rocklin, CA: Prima Publishing and Communications, 1988), dedication page.
4. "The Central Link," Central Wesleyan Church Newsletter Vol. 2, No. 2, Feb. 1990, Holland, MI, p. 3.
5. Glenn and Nelsen, *Raising Self-Reliant Children*, p. 23.
6. Glenn and Nelsen, *Raising Self-Reliant Children*.
7. Bob Benson, *Laughter in the Walls* (Nashville: Impact Books, 1969).
8. Glenn and Nelsen, *Raising Self-Reliant Children*, p. 29.
9. Robert Fulghum, "All I Ever Really Needed to Know I Learned in Kindergarten," *All I Ever Really Needed to Know I Learned in Kindergarten* (New York: Ballantine Books, 1986), pp. 4-6.

Chapter 6—Caring Through Eliminating Home Messies
1. Emilie Barnes, *Survival for Busy Women* (Eugene, OR: Harvest House Pub., 1988).
2. Wirt and Bechstrom, *Topical Encyclopedia*, p. 42.
3. Ibid., p. 22.

Chapter 7—When Women Care to Reach Out
1. Emilie Barnes and Sue Gregg, *Holiday Menus for Busy Women* (Riverside, CA: Eating Better Publications, 1989), p. 46.
2. Emilie Barnes and Sue Gregg, *The Busy Woman's Breakfast Book* (Riverside, CA: Eating Better Publications, 1989), p. 39.
3. Ibid., p. 57.

Chapter 8—Meeting the Needs of the Heart
1. Lauren Littauer Briggs, *What You Can Say . . . When You Don't Know What to Say* (Eugene, OR: Harvest House Publishers, 1985), pp. 80-82.
2. Ibid., pp. 150-55.
3. *Our Daily Bread*, Feb. 29, 1984 (Grand Rapids, MI: Radio Bible Class).

Chapter 9—When Women Care About Hospitality
1. Recommended hospitality books to read: *The Gracious Woman* by June Curtis (Harvest House Pub.), and *Creative Hospitality* by Marlene LeFever (Tyndale House).

Chapter 10—Caring Through Friendship
1. Alice Waugh Moore, *There Are Words of Friendship* (Lombard, IL: Great Quotations Inc., 1989), p. 1.